"Even the healthiest marriage can face the shell shock of an unexpected challenge that life throws at us from outside the relationship. Unemployment. Parenting struggles. Death. The unimaginable. Long-married couples Gene and Carol Kent and David and Cindy Lambert know well the churned-up waters of such storms. *Staying Power* offers insights, skills, and clear direction that equip a couple to respond to trials in a way that strengthens their marriage. Rather than being torn apart, couples can discover how to move forward together and build staying power into their marriages."

Elisa Morgan, speaker; author, *The Prayer Coin, The Beauty of Broken*, and *Hello, Beauty Full*; cohost, Discover the Word, www.discovertheword.org

"This powerful book is, in a word, *real*. No simple platitudes or pat answers here. You'll find real people filled with real emotions sharing real situations and offering real solutions. Every pastor, counselor, teacher, and therapist needs this resource on their shelves. The crisis helpsheets alone are a gold mine of information. Even happily married, no-problems-at-our-house couples should read *Staying Power* for the many practical ideas for strengthening communication skills with your spouse. And for any couple going through life's most difficult trials, this is the read you need right now. You won't find wiser, more compassionate friends than Carol, Gene, Cindy, and Dave. Their sound, biblical direction will help you and your marriage partner press through the hard times and emerge stronger than ever. Whatever unexpected challenge has landed on your doorstep, *Staying Power* has the answers you've been looking for."

Liz Curtis Higgs, bestselling author of *Bad Girls of the Bible*

"Looking for the superglue that can hold your love together when life tries to pull you apart? Want a shelter from the storm you and your mate find yourselves in? Do you desire to grow stronger, closer, more intimate in your marriage year after year? The Kents and Lamberts have lived and loved through some of life's most difficult circumstances yet are stronger, more resilient, closer, and more in love, and you can be too! *Staying Power* is the GPS directing you to long-lasting love."

Pam and Bill Farrel, codirectors of Love-Wise.com, authors of bestselling *Men Are Like Waffles—Women Are Like Spaghetti* and *Red-Hot Monogamy*

"Marriage isn't always easy, and in today's 'disposable' society we throw relationships away too easily when life gets hard. There's another way, though, and that way is discussed in the pages of this book. If you're ready to let the pain in your life give fresh purpose to your marriage, dig in and let the Kents and the Lamberts show you the way."

Mark and Jill Savage, authors of *No More Perfect Marriages*, www.NoMorePerfectMarriages.com

"When the loss of a child or some other crisis jolts your life and rocks your marriage, this book will become your personal page-turner, showing you how you and your mate can pull together not only to survive but to thrive."

Linda Evans Shepherd, author of *When You Need to Move a Mountain*

"All couples will struggle with crises that are not of their making and are beyond their control, but not all will survive. In *Staying Power* the Kents and Lamberts give invaluable tools to not only survive a crisis but thrive in the relationship.

By not ignoring the land mines that can blow up a marriage but strategically disarming them, *Staying Power* shows us how to maneuver the unfamiliar terrain of uncertainty that comes with a crisis and grow stronger through it. The stories will encourage you. The practical helps will empower you. A must-read book for all couples."

Sharon Jaynes, bestselling author of *Praying for Your Husband from Head to Toe* and *Lovestruck*

"How I wish we had this unique book on marriage some years ago when we had a series of crises! Life happens to all of us in one way or another, but through intention and understanding, we can choose to grow closer instead of letting life tear us apart. This unique book shows us how. The Kents and Lamberts write with gracious authority, as they have been there. Out of their experiences, they have written a wise and helpful book to offer insightful strategies for real-life couples on how to stay together when the world throws its worst at them. What a fabulous and helpful book for your own marriage or to give as a gift to a couple who needs its message of staying power."

Bill and Nancie Carmichael, authors of *Lord, Bless My Child*; *Lord, Bless This Marriage*; *Habits of a Healthy Home*; and *The Unexpected Power of Home*

"We team-teach at writers' conferences all across the country. Life crises do not take a break while you're on the road. These crises can either tear your marriage apart or knit you together. The Kents and Lamberts give us hope that we are not marital frauds; we're just flawed partners committed to Christ and to each other."

Suzanne and Shawn Kuhn, Brookstone Creative Group

"This book needs to be in the hands of every married couple and of those considering marriage. Life is difficult and marriage is complicated. Gene and Carol Kent and Dave and Cindy Lambert have written a masterpiece for couples! Filled with practical principles as well as authentic stories, this book will show you exactly how to discover staying power in your marriage."

Steve and Becky Harling, international conference speakers and authors of *Listen Well, Lead Better*

STAYING *Power*

STAYING *Power*

BUILDING A STRONGER MARRIAGE WHEN LIFE SENDS ITS WORST

CAROL AND GENE KENT
CINDY AND DAVID LAMBERT

a division of Baker Publishing Group
Grand Rapids, Michigan

Published by Revell
a division of Baker Publishing Group
PO Box 6287, Grand Rapids, MI 49516-6287
www.revellbooks.com

Printed in the United States of America

Library of Congress Cataloging-in-Publication Data
Names: Kent, Carol, 1947– author.
Title: Staying power : building a stronger marriage when life sends its worst / Carol and Gene Kent, Cindy and David Lambert.
Description: Grand Rapids, Michigan : Revell, a division of Baker Publishing Group, 2020. | Includes bibliographical references.
Identifiers: LCCN 2019036338 | ISBN 9780800737054 (paperback)
Subjects: LCSH: Marriage—Religious aspects—Christianity.
Classification: LCC BV835 .K46165 2020 | DDC 248.8/44—dc23
LC record available at https://lccn.loc.gov/2019036338

20 21 22 23 24 25 26 7 6 5 4 3 2 1

Carol and Gene
dedicate our work on this book
to our parents:

To Bruce and Rhua Bliss,
Gene's mom and stepfather, a couple who loved each other through their challenges and cuddled together every night for forty-two years before Bruce left for heaven in 2012.

To Clyde and Pauline Afman,
married sixty-two years and now together in heaven. You reminded us that a good marriage takes steadfast love, forgiveness, and hard work.

Cindy and Dave
dedicate our work on this book
to the parents whose example shines through
any insights we've gained about marriage:

To Scott and Hazel Lambert,
who celebrated their seventieth wedding anniversary just before they passed away in 2015. Growing up, I heard you disagree, but I never heard you speak to each other in anger.

To Millard and Dolores Thomas,
married sixty-five years and counting, thank you for being a living example of loyal, steadfast, persevering love.

Contents

A Note to the Reader

"It's almost midnight," Dave said.

Carol, Gene, and Cindy all groaned. "Already?"

"How is that possible?"

"Where did the day go?"

The four of us had been together since noon sharing stories, laughing, wiping tears, and comparing notes for almost twelve hours, yet none of us wanted our time together to end. We saw each other only twice each year. Once over dinner at the annual International Christian Retail Show and once for a day during Carol and Gene's annual vacation in west Michigan not far from Dave and Cindy's home.

"It's such an encouragement," Carol said, "to spend time with another couple who has weathered the storms of life and lived to laugh about it."

"We could fill a book with the truths we discussed today," Gene joked.

"Maybe we will someday," Dave said.

That was a decade ago, and we finally did it!

Our vision for *Staying Power* was to write to couples who, like us, were encountering the many challenges that life throws our way, yet were determined to use those challenges to make our marriages stronger rather than see them weakened or left faltering. We'd all grieved over friends' marriages that hadn't made it after the loss of a child or a health crisis or a financial meltdown or, or, or . . . the list goes on and on. We weren't talking about the kinds of challenges that come from *inside* a marriage, like infidelity or addiction to pornography or gambling or substance abuse. We were talking about the stressors that come from *outside* the marriage, like having a son incarcerated or raising a grandchild or dealing with a life-threatening illness.

The four of us compared notes on what made the difference between couples whose marriages grew stronger in such crises and couples who didn't make it. What choices and behaviors built us up through the hard times? What fed our relationships when life sent its worst? What great examples from the marriages of others had we seen that had inspired us to persevere and grow deeper during the tough times? We began posing that question to other couples and heard some fascinating stories that offered principles to explore and examples to follow.

We all four agreed that the crises we and others had endured made our marriages deeper rather than weaker when we responded with the practices that now make up our table of contents.

Dave tells this story:

Years ago, my good friend and backpacking buddy Ross Campbell and I decided to write a book together (*Getting a Clue in a Clueless World*).[1] As we wrote, we liked to find quiet places and hole up for a few days together, mostly writing individually during the day and then getting together in the evening to share ideas and review each other's work.

During one of those evening sessions, parked in front of a roaring fireplace at a Residence Inn in Michigan, Ross said, "I've got a story that might make a good anecdote for the book, from when I was in the navy. Ours was one of the ships blockading Cuba during the Cuban missile crisis. I thought we were going to start World War III!"

I listened with rapt attention, and it was truly a great story—and we did use it. That reminded me of something: "So, my senior year in high school, my friends and I loved the outdoors, just as I do now. Two of my best friends and I took my friend's Corvair station wagon, some cans of chili, an ice chest, and my brother's guitar on a weekend camping trip out into the desert. It was my turn to drive—and I accidently drove that Corvair right off a cliff! Totaled the car, but fortunately I didn't total any of the three of us. It was close."

And on we went, sharing stories from our own past of the difficult, the painful, the humiliating, the costly, the sorrowful. In most of those stories, we didn't look too good.

"But the truth is," I said when the flow of stories slowed, "I am who I am because of those events. Some of them were mistakes on my part, including some real lulus. And others, like my leukemia, were things that happened *to* me. They hurt. They cost me plenty. But the lessons I learned through them, the truths about myself and others they revealed, shaped me. Talk about trial by fire!"

Ross nodded. And then it struck both of us at the same time. "How ironic," he said, "that the events that we claim were the formative and absolutely necessary events of our lives, the things that made us the men we are today, as embarrassing and regrettable and sometimes horrifying as those things might be, are *exactly* the kind of thing we're working so hard to protect our own kids from ever experiencing! *Of course* we're trying to protect them! What father wouldn't? And yet without the *trials and tribulations* the Bible promised us, will our kids grow up strong and wise and persistent? And maybe that's why we're promised those trials and tribulations, for just that reason—to strengthen us and give us endurance and wisdom and perspective."

We think Ross was right. Think of the kinds of crises we're talking about in this book, the kind of difficult life experiences that strike a marriage: the loss of a loved one, an adoption gone awry, a family member's addiction to drugs or alcohol, infertility, a natural disaster that causes you to lose everything. As painful as those things may be, as challenging and disruptive to your lives as they indeed are, as Ross pointed out, those things can make us who we are. Or in this case, those things can make our marriages what they are.

Your marriage *will* face trials and tribulations. They can defeat you. They can cause you to give up. They can drive you apart and spell the end of your marriage. They can drive you to turn on each other in a rage. Or . . . they can cause you to pull together as a unit, a team committed to facing this challenge together and emerging from it in the end closer and more committed to each other than ever, and knowing each other better than you ever thought it possible to know another human being.

The truth is, the choice is yours—yours together. We can't make it for you, but what we can do is discuss with you—even as we share some of the embarrassing and painful stories from our own past and some stories of other couples we know and admire—the ways you can arm yourselves to face those challenges, when they come, with wisdom and strength. The ways you can give your marriage staying power.

Join us on that journey.

The stories in this book are all true. In some cases, they are our stories—the stories of the Kents and the Lamberts. In other cases, they are the true stories of other couples who allowed us to identify them by name. And there are also stories of couples who asked us to change their names and some of the details of their experiences to protect their privacy and that of their family. Some of the stories are dramatic and unusual, as you'll see. And some will sound very much like the everyday things you experience in your marriage. Whether their names appear in this book or not, we feel a great sense of gratitude and admiration for those couples who, despite the pain and the difficult memories, were willing to share with us—and now with you—some of the most difficult episodes of their marriages.

We've been fascinated and edified by these stories—and we're sure you will be too.

CHAPTER 1

We're in This Together . . . or Not

> Marriage is like a three-legged race: Try to push ahead without your partner's cooperation, and you both fall. Work together, and you both do well.
>
> —Dr. Steve Stephens

When the phone rang, it sounded just as it did on any other day. Chad and his second wife, Chloe, had been married for only a couple of years. It hadn't been easy. Blending a family never is, and they had each brought children into this marriage. When Chad picked up the receiver, he had no idea that this call would introduce one of their marriage's toughest trials.

"Chad," his dad's voice said, ragged and hoarse. "I have bad news. We lost Wyatt."

Wyatt was Chad's little brother, the sweet but wayward and aimless thirtysomething baby of the family. Then followed several minutes of silence while neither could find voice to speak, but Chad's grief must have been clear on his face because Chloe, alarmed, stopped emptying the dishwasher and stood watching him.

When the call was over, Chad didn't flee into Chloe's arms for comfort, as many of us would have. A private person, Chad dealt with his grief and confusion privately; he shakily recounted the news to Chloe, then retreated to their bedroom and closed the door before he allowed himself to surrender to the grief of losing his baby brother. He didn't emerge for a half hour or so, and as soon as he did a close friend arrived, alerted by Chloe, and he and Chad wandered through the adjacent woods for a while and talked. It was another day or two before Chad and Chloe, their emotions already testy toward each other because of the stress of their uneasy marriage, could talk in any depth about the loss of Wyatt, and even then Chad remained emotionally closed off, bearing his grief inside.

Slapping the Mattress

Then came the flight across several states to join Chad's parents for the funeral. One night in the spare room at his parents' house, Chad was trying to quiet his emotions long enough to get to sleep when a loud noise made him sit up in alarm. It was Chloe; she had slapped the mattress, loudly enough that Chad wondered if she had awakened his parents, just two rooms away. "Don't you understand that this is hard on me too?" she said. "I've lost a family member as well! And I feel like I'm just baggage to you in all this, like I'm useful only for making sure the coffee's made and the napkins and silverware are laid out. Doesn't my presence here matter? I feel invisible to you!"

Chad tried to clear his head and understand. "I just buried my little brother," he said finally. "I know you're trying to do all you can, but is it so hard to understand that I don't have the emotional reserve right now to affirm you for it?"

She nodded sadly in the dim light from the night-light. Chad rolled over and seemed to go back to sleep. "All I got was his back," Chloe said later, "as usual. He just kind of disappears when things get hard. Me, I tossed and turned the rest of the night—and to make matters worse, I felt guilty about what I'd just said to him, which in retrospect sounded selfish."

Chad would remember that night just three years later when, feeling rundown and headachy, he went to his doctor only to receive a diagnosis of cancer. He was admitted to the hospital immediately. In the second week of that month-long stay, still plagued by the debilitating headaches brought on by his cancer and still physically weak and far from sure that he would beat this—his doctor, after all, had said that this form of cancer was incurable and gave him two years, tops—Chad was lying in his hospital bed with eyes closed while Chloe sat in the chair next to his bed reading. Then the mattress shifted, and Chad opened his eyes to see that Chloe had sat down on his mattress next to him. "This is incredibly hard," she said.

"On everyone else as well as me, I realize," he said, thinking of Chloe, but also of his children, of his parents.

"Do you? Do you realize that I'm afraid that I might lose my husband?" she said. "I lost my first husband to divorce, and now I might lose you to cancer! A divorcée and a widow before I'm thirty-five! I'm afraid! I don't know what's going to happen to me and to the kids if you die."

Chad tried to listen as she went on, his head throbbing so hard that sometimes he couldn't hear her, and his ever-present nausea making him glance at his bedside table to make sure a basin was nearby. And then a loud noise made him jump and drove a spike of pain through his head.

Chloe had slapped the mattress.

"I have no idea what you are thinking and feeling!" she said. "You lie there and disappear into your own head and ignore me, just when we need each other the most. I want to face this together, but instead it feels like we're each all alone."

Chad knew that something was being required of him at that moment, so adjusting his hospital gown and IV lines, he slipped his legs out of bed and sat beside her on the mattress and put his arm around her shoulders and pulled her close. He tried to find words to provide her with the togetherness she sought, but he knew that his rambling, fever-muddled words were awkward and probably unhelpful.

Any Significant Stresses?

Chad recovered. After chemo, he even managed to achieve remission, despite his doctor's dire words. A few years later, he and Chloe decided to spend time with a marriage counselor in an attempt to reverse their marriage's downhill slide.

"Have there been significant stresses on your marriage?" the counselor asked in one of their early sessions with him.

"Probably no more than usual," Chad said. He and Chloe sat silently. "Well—my brother died suddenly," Chad said after a pause. "Car crash."

"I'd say that's pretty significant," the counselor said.

"Don't forget my dad," Chloe said. She turned to the counselor. "He died from a stroke. It was horrible. Then there was Chad's cancer. He almost died. He was in treatment for a few years."

"Wait—you had cancer?" the counselor asked.

"And I got fired from my job," Chad said. "Very unpleasant—got a new boss, and there was lots of anger and back-alley maneuvering at work. Fortunately I found an even better job, but I was out of work for a few months first." He turned to Chloe. "And your brother—his alcoholism and the way he used to treat your parents."

"And your ex," Chloe said. "She made things as hard on us as she could, trying to turn the kids against us." She reached for the box of tissues. "Every summer vacation, every holiday, were impossible to negotiate, and you never stood up to her."

It took the two of them five minutes just to list all of the significant stresses on their marriage—stresses brought on not because of things that either of them had chosen or said or done. Rather, these were all things life threw at them, like cancer or the loss of a job or the death of a loved one, things imposed on their lives through no choice of their own. Their only real choice had been how to deal with them. And in their case, they had not dealt well. Each crisis brought out not the best in them but the worst, and each blamed the other for that.

By the time they finished, the counselor was shaking his head. "The wonder is not that you're in here struggling with your marriage," he said. "The wonder is that you're still married at all."

But of course, many couples face these and even worse issues and still manage to have long and satisfying marriages. What's the difference? What enables some marriages to press through these problems and emerge stronger than ever, while other marriages, like Chad and Chloe's, are weakened by their crises? No matter how wise and resilient the marriage partners, problems such as these will test them, sometimes beyond the breaking point.

The emotional barriers Chad erected around himself were always his first line of defense, and any significant stress brought them out. Normally a hard worker who tried to make sure everyone's needs were met, during times of stress Chad tended to sulk. Likewise, Chloe's narcissism, her tendency to interpret everything that happened in their lives through the lens of her own emotional needs, was her first response, exacerbated not only by stressors like sickness or financial problems but also by Chad's withdrawal from her at those times.

What choices and behaviors could Chad and Chloe make in the midst of their crises that could make their future brighter and give their marriage the staying power it needed to not only survive but thrive?

Staying Power

Unforeseen pressures hit our marriages when we least expect them. Your newborn has a severe disability. An accident or illness permanently impairs the health of your spouse. You discover that your teenager has become addicted to drugs or alcohol. Job loss rocks your financial foundation. An aging parent moves into your home. Your son is diagnosed with ADHD. You experience another miscarriage when you desperately long for a child.

Is it possible to build a stronger marriage when you face a challenge that doesn't go away even though you pray together and ask God to give you wisdom? Why do some marriages fall apart when life pulls savagely at them while other couples develop a stronger bond in the face of insurmountable external pressures?

Many of the crises that can tear a marriage apart arise from decisions or character issues of one or both of the marriage partners: infidelity, betrayal, pornography addiction, and so many more. But those are not the crises we're talking about in *Staying Power*. There are many fine books that address those devastating situations. This book addresses the choices, practices, and principles that can make a marriage stronger when faced with the types of crises that come from *outside* the marriage through no choice of the husband or wife—life crises that we all are hit with at some point. For example, in addition to the things we've already listed, crises such as infertility, a disabled child, the loss of a child, a health challenge, the addiction or incarceration of a loved one, a wayward child or adult child in crisis, the need to raise a grandchild, the death of a friend or loved one, an adoption gone awry, and so on.

No matter what the external crisis, is it possible that there are choices, principles, and insights that not only can equip your marriage to endure such an onslaught of circumstances, but actually leave your marriage stronger and more resilient and closer and more vibrant than it was before the crisis hit? We believe it is!

Let's hear from a couple who faced horrific circumstances and made different decisions than Chad and Chloe—decisions that strengthened their relationship rather than weakened it.

Everything Changed in a Moment—Carol and Gene's Story

The phone rang in the middle of the night. I (Carol) looked at the clock—12:35 a.m. Still groggy, I saw Gene pick up the receiver, then watched as a look of shock and horror transformed his face. Choking back tears, he looked at me and said, "That was Jason's wife. He was just arrested for the murder of her ex-husband. He's in jail in Orlando."

I had never been in shock like this before. Nausea swept over me. I tried to get out of bed, but my legs wouldn't hold my weight. Thoughts swirled: *Our son is a graduate of the US Naval Academy. He's a husband, stepfather to two beautiful little girls. He's never been in trouble before. This must be a horrible dream. I'll soon wake up and find out everything is okay.*

But everything wasn't okay.

After he hung up the phone—and over and over again for the next days and weeks and months—Gene and I reviewed our recollections of Jason's phone calls during his first year of marriage. Clearly, there had been a problem, a more serious one than we'd noticed at the time. In those phone conversations, instead of talking about global concerns, breaking news, and his work with the navy, Jason had repeatedly expressed his fear for the safety of his two stepdaughters, three and six years old at the time. Despite the multiple allegations of abuse against their biological father, it appeared that he would get unsupervised visitation with them. Jason was about to leave on his first military assignment outside the continental US, in Hawaii, and during that time the girls might spend as much as six weeks of visitation with their biological father during the summer. Jason had begun unraveling—mentally, emotionally, and spiritually—as he fixated on what might happen to those two precious girls. And now our twenty-five-year-old son had done the unthinkable. He had shot and killed his wife's ex-husband.

Better Days

Just two weeks earlier, Gene and I had walked hand-in-hand along the St. Clair River in Port Huron, Michigan, where we lived. The trees were dressed in their full fall splendor in varying shades of red, yellow, and orange. It was a sunny day, and the temperature was refreshingly brisk. The sky reflected vividly in the river, as if bragging about the grandeur of the Blue Water Area and the famous bridge that connected our city in Michigan with Sarnia, Ontario, Canada. The scene would have made the ideal promotional postcard for the Port Huron Chamber of Commerce. We chatted about the season of life we were entering—with a grown, married son, a lovely daughter-in-law, and two adorable step-granddaughters. We were traveling in ministry. I was speaking at Christian conferences, and Gene was managing the business part of ministry. Life was good. A sense of deep joy and happiness enveloped us. I looked up at him and said, "Does life get any better than this?"

Little did we know.

After the phone call and throughout the rest of the night, Gene and I intermittently sobbed, held each other, prayed, and started making a list of tasks and concerns. We had to contact relatives and close friends. We needed an attorney. We feared for our son's safety. Our daughter-in-law and the girls needed to be moved from Panama City, where Jason had been in the most intensive dive school the navy offered on mixed gasses at great ocean depths. Did that have anything to do with his aberrant behavior? Thoughts swirled and emotions of fear, shock, and panic consumed us. Occasionally we simply stopped and reminded ourselves, "Breathe. Do the next thing."

Gene's Journal

Like many other English majors, I (Gene) found it easier to process my feelings in written form. I pulled out a journal that had been languishing on a bookshelf and began to chronicle what was happening.

October 25—We received the news that J.P. [Jason Paul] was arrested. Cried. Found an attorney.

October 26—Coped poorly. Cried. I am so afraid for my son.

October 27—Carol and I go through the motions of being alive, but inside we are dying.

October 28—I started reading the Bible over again, beginning in Genesis. I must have missed something in my earlier readings.

October 29—There it was in Genesis 28. Jacob is in a dream and he sees a ladder that stretches from earth to heaven. There are angels going up and down on that ladder. Jacob awakens, more alert than he's ever been before, as he becomes aware of what we face in the *visible* and in the *invisible* worlds. He sees the satanic forces of evil, but he's equally aware of the power of God. Then I read: "Surely the LORD is in this place, and I was not aware of it" (Gen. 28:16). I bowed my head and prayed, *Thank you, Father, for your comfort in the middle of this crisis.*

Headlines That Hurt

The news of the murder and Jason's arrest immediately showed up in the *Orlando Sentinel*, but it took a few weeks to reach our local Port Huron papers. Few locals knew of the tragedy. We had talked to our pastor, coworkers, relatives, and closest friends, but the general public had no idea of the crisis shaking our lives to the core.

Then a local editor from the Port Huron *Times Herald* called three times, requesting comments from the parents of the accused. We didn't return the calls, but the voicemail messages the editor left warned us that the news would be all over the city the following day. Gene and I went to bed that night feeling the knots in our stomach growing tighter.

The following day's headline was devastating:

Former Port Huron Man Faces Murder Charge

A Port Huron native and Naval Academy graduate could face up to life in prison and possibly the death penalty in

> the shooting death of his wife's ex-husband outside a busy Orlando, Florida, restaurant last month.
>
> Jason Paul Kent, 25, is expected to be charged Tuesday at an Orange County Jail with . . . murder.[1]

Facing a Choice

Our marriage faced new challenges. Our distress over Jason left us short-tempered, and we sometimes allowed little disagreements to escalate into full-blown arguments. Those disagreements sometimes involved money: How would we ever afford the huge retainer for the highly recommended attorney we were considering? Should we empty our retirement accounts? Would we have to sell our home?

At other times, the awkwardness between us was over intimacy. I (Carol) couldn't even think of actually enjoying the pleasure of making love with my husband while my son was in jail awaiting trial. Gene, on the other hand, believed if we ever needed the release and the closeness of physical intimacy, it was now.

One thing was certain: regardless of how we felt, we had to keep working in ministry in order not just to pay our general living expenses but to afford the attorney we hired.

Three weeks after Jason's arrest, we were in Germany where I was speaking at a US military wives' conference. Our anxiety was dialed way up to high. We hadn't told the meeting planner or any of the committee members that our son had been arrested for murder. My speaking and writing ministry was our only source of income, so whether I felt like it or not, we had to continue fulfilling my commitments as a public speaker in order to pay for Jason's defense. I was the keynote speaker on each of the five days of this event, but there was time to relax for a while each afternoon. Still struggling with jet lag, we lay down for a nap. I felt Gene's hand touch the small of my back. Then he gently caressed my shoulders and made his way down to my thighs, my calves, and finally my feet. I felt the warmth of his love and was aware of his patience in waiting for me to be ready to respond to his overt expressions of love.

Our bodies began responding to the God-given rhythms of the intimacy and love we had spent years nurturing with each other, and after we had consummated this precious, holy experience, we both burst into tears. Why? One reason was that we both knew that our son, apart from a miracle of mercy, would never again experience what we had just enjoyed.

From that point forward, we were both aware that we had a choice to make. Would we allow the stress of our son's incarceration to tear us apart? Or would we stay together—no matter what—and learn how to let this experience make us not weaker but stronger? (For the whole story, see Carol's book *When I Lay My Isaac Down*.)[2]

In It Together

Remember Chad and Chloe? They could have fallen into the kind of behavior that would destroy a marriage. Feeling that her husband didn't support her or even really see her, Chloe could have given in to the temptation of an affair with some new love who would be totally fascinated by her and give her all the attention he was able to give (when he wasn't with his wife). Chad could have given in to the despair that often comes with such trials as losing a close family member or being diagnosed with a serious illness and sought solace in alcohol or drugs. Either could have reached the point of being so fed up with their spouse that their rage boiled over into abusive behavior. All those things could have happened—but they didn't.

Their struggle resulted from an inability to cope productively with the attacks neither had sought. Fortunately, they finally realized they lacked the coping techniques to defend their marriage when the evils of life began to rip it apart. They found the strength and commitment to move forward *together*.

How *could* they have defended their marriage more effectively from the start of the crisis? What choices and skills enable some couples to weather such crises successfully, while others falter and even crumble?

Ecclesiastes 4:9–12 is often quoted during wedding ceremonies:

> Two are better than one,
>   because they have a good return for their labor:
> If either of them falls down,
>   one can help the other up.
> But pity anyone who falls
>   and has no one to help them up.
> Also, if two lie down together, they will keep warm.
>   But how can one keep warm alone?
> Though one may be overpowered,
>   two can defend themselves.
> A cord of three strands is not quickly broken.

How, exactly, are we to do that? When a crisis hits and both are stunned, how can one help the other up? When life is tearing you apart from one another, how is it possible that "*if two lie down together, they will keep warm*"? When both spouses are stretched to their limits, running on empty, and completely out of touch with what their spouse is thinking and feeling, how is it that "*two can defend themselves*"?

Clearly, for the plan revealed in Ecclesiastes to work, a married couple needs the Lord to be central in their lives, for him to complete that cord of three strands. So are there specific choices, strategies, and techniques that a couple can discover and practice, with the Lord's help, that will give them staying power when life throws its worst at them?

We believe there are.

Even better, we believe that if a couple grows experienced in these staying-power practices, not only can their marriage survive the crises of life but it can also grow stronger through them.

In *Staying Power,* we're going to present the choices and techniques and attitudes that we and other couples we know have experienced that will enable you to create a strategy for surviving the hand grenades that threaten your marriage, whether you're trying to dig your way out of the bomb crater that the detonation just tossed you into or hoping to put a strategy in place *before* the grenade explodes. These ideas are the things that worked for us and others—or in some cases, the ideas that we wish we'd put in place and that would have made our lives much easier if we had!

We will present twelve separate strategies and skillsets—one in each of twelve chapters. And the first one, in this chapter, is simple. It's the chapter title: we're in this together.

A couple does not defeat a difficult life crisis by each angrily separating himself or herself from the other and trying to handle the crisis alone, resisting whatever efforts are made by the other. It doesn't work that way. It didn't work for Chad and Chloe, and it won't work for you.

Chad and Chloe's marriage was threatened in the face of a multitude of crises not because of all the things they did wrong, but because they didn't know how to do the important things right. And the most important was this: In crisis after crisis, they were the opposite of "in it together." They were far apart. They slipped into grumbling rather than supporting their spouse with their whole heart. Fortunately, once they got help and committed themselves to some of the practices we discuss in this book, they were able to stop their downward spiral and begin rebuilding their marriage—but only because they recognized that *during* their crises they had damaged their relationship, and it now required healing. Their cord had been frayed. They had repair work to do.

Carol and Gene, on the other hand, decided from the beginning that they would not survive the devastating crisis they faced unless they faced it together. Unless each had the other's back. Unless each helped the other up when they fell (which they certainly would). Unless they lay down together and each kept the other warm. Unless each contributed steadfastly their own cord to combine with that of their partner and the Lord to create a threefold cord that would withstand the power of this crisis and all other crises. Unless together they lived out Ecclesiastes 4:9–12.

This requires a together-come-what-may, for-better-or-worse, in-sickness-and-in-health, for-richer-for-poorer kind of commitment. It's the commitment you already made once, and it's the one you have to recommit to now as the hurricanes of life sweep over your marriage, over your family. Otherwise your marriage will follow the pattern of Chad and Chloe, not the pattern of Carol and Gene and the many other couples you will meet over the course of this book, couples who fought back against their crises together and survived.

The simple truth is that life can pull the rug out from under your marriage. The enemy who prowls about like a roaring lion looking for someone to devour is endlessly creative in finding ways to knock us down. Because, after all, if we're spending all our time and energy trying to get back on our feet again from one setback after another, we'll not have the energy or the concentration to look for the ways God wants us to grow and flourish—in life and in marriage.

However, we are loved by the God who tells us this:

> Consider it pure joy, my brothers and sisters, whenever you face trials of many kinds, because you know that the testing of your faith produces perseverance. Let perseverance finish its work so that you may be mature and complete, not lacking anything. If any of you lacks wisdom, you should ask God, who gives generously to all without finding fault, and it will be given to you. (James 1:2–5)

The four of us have discovered through God's faithfulness during our own trials that as distressing as many of the sudden challenges our marriages face are, they're also a rich opportunity. An opportunity to grow together in strength and in wisdom. An opportunity to be a source of light for everyone else in the midst of that horrible circumstance. And yes, even an opportunity to make our marriages stronger, more resilient than before the crisis hit. That's what happens when you approach a crisis together, of one mind, bound together in a threefold cord.

Jesus gives us a promise in John 16:33—"In this world you will have trouble. But take heart! I have overcome the world." There is no doubt that we can expect life to continue to make things difficult for us. In whatever way it can, and as often as it can.

But our faith lies in the one who has overcome the world. Let's turn to scripturally sound insights, skills, and clear direction that will equip us to respond to trials in a way that strengthens rather than weakens our marriage.

Let's discover the secrets of staying power.

Discussion Questions
for Couples and Small Groups

1. What was your main take-away from this chapter?
2. Each of you individually make a list of the five most trying crises you have experienced since your wedding. Compare lists with your spouse—you may be surprised at what your spouse does or doesn't include on the list. Rank the crises in terms of how difficult and painful each was for you. If you are reading this in a group study, each couple pick one to share with the group.
3. Based on what you know of Chad and Chloe's marriage from the brief story in the chapter, identify some of the mistakes they made in their marriage.

What could they have done differently to build a stronger marriage before and during their crisis?

4. "Chad and Chloe's marriage was threatened in the face of a multitude of crises not because of all the things they did wrong," this chapter says, "but because they didn't know how to do the important things right." Given what you've learned in this chapter, what are some of the important things that you'd like to do right in your marriage when a crisis strikes? What are some of the things you saw in this chapter that Carol and Gene were doing right?
5. Shortly after receiving news of their son's arrest, Gene read in Genesis 28:16, "Surely the LORD is in this place, and I was not aware of it." It reminded him that God was at work in their lives even when they couldn't see it. Can you think of times and ways in which God was at work in your life, in the midst of your crises, and you weren't aware of it until later?

CHAPTER 2

Make the Next Right Choice

> Just do the next thing you're reasonably certain Jesus wants you to do. (And commit to it immediately—in the next ten seconds—before you change your mind!)
>
> —Clare De Graaf, *The 10-Second Rule*

"You wouldn't believe it," Carrie said. "She's been spending every night, alone, in a rat- and roach-infested basement, while Troy and Katie go out every night selling drugs. And this is in a drug house! Anybody who wanders into that house to buy drugs could go down into the basement, find her, and molest her. Who's to stop them? Not her parents, because they're not even there—they're out using and selling drugs. A seven-year-old girl alone in a place like that! She's terrified all night long. She told me. Brad, we can't just leave her there. We can't. It would be a violation of everything we believe, of everything we are."

So, finally, it had come to this. Brad and Carrie had been keeping close tabs on the welfare of their granddaughter Paige ever since she was born, seven years before.

Seven years of Carrie checking Troy and Katie's refrigerator whenever she was in Cleveland and finding nothing nutritious to eat. Seven years of taking Katie grocery shopping at Brad and Carrie's expense so that Paige would have a reasonably healthy diet at home—but knowing that just because you buy the food doesn't mean it's going to get prepared before it rots.

Seven years of arranging for preschool classes for Paige and setting up transportation to those classes so that she would have exposure to other kids and to supportive adults.

Seven years of convincing Troy to enter rehab for his drug habit—only to have Katie show up at his rehab before he had completed it and talk him into pulling out early.

Seven years of throwing money into Troy and Katie's cars and their housing and their medical care with no confidence that the cars would be maintained, the apartments wouldn't be trashed, or the instructions of the doctors would be followed.

Seven years of Carrie and Brad discussing, over and over, the elephant in the room: When would Paige's situation as the daughter of dysfunctional, law-breaking, substance-abusing parents become so risky, so dangerous for a young child, that as her grandparents they would have to step in and take over Paige's care? They had come so close so many times, only to pull back and say, *She loves her mom and dad, and she's not going to want to be separated from them. The best thing for everybody is if they can get their act together and straighten up—which they probably will, at some point. Let's help them one more time. Let's give them one more chance.*

And one more chance, and one more. Was it the accumulative weight of all the arrests, the disturbing things Paige said about her life with her parents, and the glazed looks and dilated pupils and slurred words her parents demonstrated one too many times that finally convinced Brad and Carrie that the time had come? Or was it the appalling conditions she found Paige in on that particular trip? Probably both.

Brad was several states away on business when he got the call from Carrie about the rat- and roach-infested basement. "So do we do this?" he asked after she had filled him in.

"Do we have a choice?" she asked.

"If the only alternative is leaving her alone night after night in the basement of a drug house, I guess not," he said.

Carrie was supposed to join him on the business trip, but instead she sat Troy and Katie down and persuaded them to let her take Paige back to Lansing with her until they could get themselves together. Tearfully, they agreed. She had them write out permission for her to take temporary legal custody of Paige so that she could enroll her in school and get medical care for her as needed. They had it notarized. Carrie drove Paige home with her, thinking it would be for a few months, just until her parents came to their senses and perhaps went through rehab.

Two weeks later, both Troy and Katie were arrested for possession with intent to sell.

Paige lived with her grandparents Carrie and Brad until she graduated from high school eleven years later.

When Brad and Carrie took on responsibility for Paige, they had no idea that it would become one of the primary shaping influences of their marriage. They had each raised children in previous marriages, and those children were now adults. And now they were starting over—and starting over with a child troubled by years of growing up with parents less mature than she was, a child who needed counseling, comforting, loads of time, and attention. And if her *childhood* was challenging, imagine the turmoil of her teenage years.

Plans Brad and Carrie had made would have to be changed. The empty-nest years would need to wait another decade. Money and time would have to be reallocated. The quiet evenings at home they looked forward to became tumultuous with their meeting the needs of a traumatized child.

How do you make it through a challenge like that? "For one thing," Brad said after they'd delivered Paige to her dorm room to begin her first year of college, "we always had the assurance that when the time of crisis came for Paige, when her needs as a small child became desperate, we made the right choice. When we heard others say, 'Well, I'm really not in favor of removing children from their parents' home,' we didn't need to waste time rethinking it. We had talked it through and talked it through for years before we finally took that huge step, and we were unshakably confident that we'd called it right. We'd made the right choice. After years of living on the edge of danger, her parents had finally crossed the line. They couldn't be counted on to make the right choices for themselves, much less for a daughter. We stepped in. And just in time—if we hadn't already had her, then after her parents' arrest Paige would probably have gone into Cleveland's child protective services system.

"Life is a series of choices. We had made the next right one."

The 10-Second Rule

Clare De Graaf was in Chicago on North Michigan Avenue when he saw a homeless man, one of the hundreds he's seen over the years. But this time, he sensed God speaking to him: Go talk to this man. Have lunch with him.

Inwardly, Clare groaned. He'd been following, for ten years, the rule of life he calls the 10-Second Rule, quoted at the beginning of this chapter: "Just do the next thing you're reasonably certain Jesus wants you to do. (And commit to it immediately—in the next ten seconds—before you change your mind!)" Even so, he still found himself reluctant to obey when the impulses God gave him took him out of his comfort zone, as this one did. But Clare had long since made a few of what he calls "pre-decisions" to guide his responses to the 10-Second Rule, and one of them was that if he was alone and he sensed God urging him to engage with a homeless person he came across, he would try to share a meal with him, or at least offer to buy him one.

> So I asked, "Are you hungry? Let me buy you lunch."
>
> "Yeah, sure," the man said without enthusiasm. I was sure he was hungry, so I just figured that he was as wary of me as I used to be of guys like him. This was new territory for both of us.
>
> Despite his initial misgivings, he ate like he was going to the chair! Between mouthfuls, he asked an obvious question: "Why does a guy like you want to have lunch with a guy like me?"
>
> Somewhat sheepishly I answered, "To be honest, I didn't. But I'm a follower of Jesus, and I'm trying to obey the 10-Second Rule."[1]

Clare's experience has been that when he responds with that line, people can't resist it—they want to know what the 10-Second Rule is, and that usually leads to a conversation about Jesus. On that day in Chicago, the man replied just as Clare had expected he would, and they ended up having a nice, long talk about Jesus, about the man's life and dreams, about where he'd gone wrong, about his scattered and fractured family—about many things.

> Was I any real help to him? I don't know. But I left that restaurant a better man than I'd been when I had entered. Like most people, I often thought of homeless panhandlers as simply a nuisance, rather than as real human beings with crushed hopes, people needing grace as badly as I do. I believe God intended that one encounter, on that day, for me—to soften my heart.[2]

That moment of ministry was made possible by Clare's decision, years before, to live by the 10-Second Rule—but it was also made possible by the *pre-decisions* he had made to respond in certain ways in certain circumstances. Once that circumstance arose, Clare didn't have to struggle with a decision about how to act. He had already decided. All he had to do was obey, to act in accordance with the plan he had already made himself. A good way to understand pre-decisions is to think of them as a way to redeem our times of failure, the times we fall far short of how we know God wants us to behave, by formulating a plan of action for the *next* time we're caught in those circumstances. Because, Clare insists, *there will be a next time!* It's a little bit like finding out which questions are likely to be on the pop quiz so that you can figure out the correct answers and be ready to give them. Except that in this case, it's something a lot more important than a grade in school—it's obeying God: "Do not withhold good from those who deserve it when it's in your power to help them" (Prov. 3:27 NLT).

The application of this principle to your marriage should be pretty obvious. We've been discussing what happens to a marriage when those inevitable intrusions from outside threaten to cut your relationship off at the knees, to throw you both into the ditch beside the road of life—one of you on one side of the road and the other on the other side. Committing yourself to following the 10-Second Rule with regard to your marriage, and making a very specific set of pre-decisions about how and when you'll respond to your spouse in their time of need, a time when they need all of the patience and attention and love and affection and forgiveness you (and only you) can extend toward them, can spell the difference between surviving this particular crisis (and the next one, and the next . . .) or becoming a statistic.

We suggest the following pre-decisions, or some very like them, depending on your particular circumstances, to help you and your spouse navigate your way through the next crisis with mutual support and real teamwork.

- *I will practice automatic forgiveness.* I realize that my spouse is no more perfect than I am—so therefore, in any crises that come our way through the rest of our lives together (as well as in the times between crises), I will *automatically* forgive my spouse's lapses, weaknesses, errors in judgment, unwise words, and flares of temper, just as I hope my spouse will forgive them in me.

- *I will tame my tongue.* My tongue has often gotten me into trouble, and therefore:
  - I will strive to make my words positive, encouraging, helpful, kind, constructive, and biblical.
  - I will be the first to apologize and the first to admit I'm wrong.
  - I will speak the truth in *love*.
  - I will not lash out in anger.
  - I will listen first, then speak when I know the facts and have thought them through.

- *I will persevere through failure.* Failure happens in life, and it will happen sometimes to us. When it does, I won't act or speak as if the sky is falling. I will work with my spouse to regroup, figure out what went wrong, and decide where we go from here. Every failure is a lesson learned, rather than the end of the world, and I will act accordingly.
- *I will respond tenderly to my spouse's needs.* When my spouse asks something of me—whether it be affection, attention, resources of some kind, time, patience, forgiveness—I will assume that the most important thing at that moment is meeting that need. When at all possible I will set aside whatever else I am doing and focus single-mindedly on my spouse's need.
- *I will not expect my spouse to read my mind.* If I feel a need for something—whether it be affection, attention, resources of some kind, time, patience, forgiveness—I will take responsibility to express that need and not assume it is already known.

- *I will accept my spouse just as he or she is.* My job is not to change my spouse but to love and honor him or her as is.
- *I will address concerns openly.* If during a crisis my spouse develops unhealthy coping mechanisms (drinking, emotionally prompted spending, unhealthy relationships, illness), I will speak up in love, take action, and seek help.
- *I will value what is important to my spouse.* If it matters to my spouse, it matters to me. If my partner suggests that we need counseling, I will keep that option open.
- *I will request and honor the advice of my spouse.* We are a team, and I will value all input from my spouse before we make a final decision.

When Life Turns Upside Down

Dan and Kirsten had just celebrated their twentieth wedding anniversary. The summer before their celebration had been magic. They'd taken their two teenage sons, Alex and Nicholas, on a trip to Italy. They'd taken part in their city's outdoor production of "A Midsummer Night's Dream." They hiked and played board games and told silly jokes. Kirsten says: "Our boys were buddies and we were a tight-knit crew. We didn't see it coming."

> In the fall, our younger son, Nicholas, started slipping in his schoolwork. He became moodier and started becoming antagonistic toward his brother. Because Alex had also gone

through a moody stage at age fourteen, we thought of the changes as something to just ride out until the hormones steadied. Instead, Nicholas worsened until that winter he admitted to us that he had been engaging in self-harm and was suffering serious depression.

In early spring, he was admitted to the hospital for the first time because he was suicidal. In our family, we call the next three years the "crisis years" because we barely had time to catch our breath between his hospitalizations. Every knife and pair of scissors and all medicine stayed in locked cabinets. We never left Nicholas home alone. We were constantly going to doctor and therapy appointments.

Most of that time, Dan and I had been an effective partnership, but stress took its toll, and I came to the end of my rope. I had nothing left to give. And Dan didn't have the resources to hold Nicholas's rope and mine too. Desperate and depleted, deeply hurt and furiously angry, I vented my emotional frustration at Dan: "I'm ready to give up. I can rebuild my happiness next to you, but not *with* you. I don't know if our relationship can be healed, and I'm not even sure I would be up for it if it could. I'm not saying we should end our marriage. I just need to be less desperately unhappy."

Kirsten's words and her vacillation between bitter coldness and hot anger pushed Dan into self-reproach and defensiveness. He withdrew.

A Series of Choices

Weeks passed. God continued to speak to Kirsten. Although she had demanded of Dan that he invest energy and effort into caring for her, she knew that, truly, her only deliverance would come from Jesus. She didn't want to cut herself off from God with hardness.

Kirsten continues:

> After a couple weeks of stubbornly stiff-arming the gentle nudges of God, I finally softened up and took action. One afternoon, sitting in my car in the grocery store parking lot, I took a deep breath and dialed.
>
> "You have reached the voicemail of M. L., family and marriage therapist. Please leave a message and I will return your call as soon as I can."
>
> With a shaky voice, I responded, "Hello, this is Kirsten Panachyda. My husband and I would like to schedule an appointment." I suddenly panicked. What was I supposed to say? "Umm . . . We're having problems and need help. I'm not sure we can even . . . Anyway, we need help. Please help us!" I hung up, trembling, embarrassed at the barely coherent message I had just left.
>
> I wasn't even sure I wanted healing in my marriage. I had moved past hurt to anger. I was ready to build my own life, with my husband as a roommate and partner but not as an intimate part of my life. The call I had just made, I knew, was not for him or for "us." I made the call as my surrender to God.
>
> The first part of healing was an angry throwing up of hands, giving up. But under God's ministration it morphed into surrender, enabling an eternal perspective and, eventually, compassion for my husband. The beginning of healing for our marriage came when I stopped looking at what Dan was or was not doing in the middle of our crisis with Nicholas. I began to focus on following Jesus.

Not knowing how long their emergency would last, Dan and Kirsten needed to figure out how to make the best choices for themselves and for their son. They eventually agreed to make three decisions:

- We will do whatever it takes.
- We will never give up.
- We will not let inconvenience destroy our marriage.

Kirsten explains:

> The third point may seem odd; it doesn't have the heroic quality of the first two. But in some ways, it was the most important. It wasn't until we acknowledged how messy, disruptive, and inconvenient a child's mental illness makes day-to-day life that we were ready to tackle the issue. We faced our selfish impulses and did the hard, time-consuming, thankless work. Making that agreement together created a strong bond and transcended conflicts over lesser decisions. We trusted each other's heart and knew that when we argued, we were only arguing over method, not vision or reliability. That decision allowed us to make each "next choice" with less stress because we trusted each other.

With the benefit of hindsight, Kirsten says that these "next right choices" are the most important ones:

1. Get help from a godly counselor—sooner rather than later.
2. Acknowledge the major stress created by caring for a child who is mentally ill or troubled in any other way

and recognize the toll it can and will take on your marriage.

3. Place your confidence in the person who can bear the weight of your expectations. And that person is not your spouse—it's Jesus.
4. Pray with honesty about your pain; write about your pain in a letter you will never send; cry and grieve over the fractures in your most important earthly relationship with your spouse; don't put on a happy face and pretend all is great; don't deny the hurt—process it.
5. Practice kindness and compassion for your spouse, especially when you don't feel like it. (Even if your spouse doesn't look like they're suffering as much as you are—they're going through the same severe stress.)
6. Confide only in those who are the cheerleaders and supporters of your marriage. Choose your close confidants with caution. When you feel like venting, be wise in what you say and to whom you say it.

After the crisis years, Nicholas began to stabilize with the help of a medication regimen, therapy, and maturity. Kirsten explains how those years affected her and Dan.

> We experienced a world of heartache, helplessness, and weariness that we could never have imagined. It took counseling, commitment to our marriage vows, and the help of the Holy Spirit to emerge from that time with our marriage intact. Today we are stronger, more compassionate, more connected to Jesus and to each other. Making the obvious next choice—to get counseling—was essential.

Before You Make Your Next Choice

As a couple, ask each other these questions:

Do we believe that God will work out our situation for our good?

I (Carol) reacted poorly when people who had just heard of our son's arrest stopped by our house, put an arm around me, and said, "And we know that all things work together for good to those who love God, to those who are the called according to His purpose" (Rom. 8:28 NKJV). I rebelled in my heart: *How can they say that so smugly? They aren't in our situation. They don't understand—and they're trying to solve our problem by stuffing a Bible verse down our throats. That makes me so angry!* And yet, even if those friends lacked tact, I needed to remember that that verse in Romans simply describes how God works. Based on everything I know about God and his Word, he *will* work this situation out for our good and his glory.

Are we willing to request advice from others?

The Bible says, "Get all the advice and instruction you can, so you will be wise the rest of your life" (Prov. 19:20 NLT). Gene and I are both firstborn, "take charge" people. Before Jason's arrest, we were used to *giving* advice, rather than *taking* it. But his arrest humbled us. We became more than willing to seek and follow wise counsel. (Well—*most* of the time.)

Have we realized there's new hope and new grace in each day?

Early in our journey with our son, I often struggled late in the day with feelings of despair and depression. But every morning, when the sun came up, my spirits were lifted. "Great is his faithfulness; his mercies begin afresh each morning" (Lam. 3:23 NLT). The choices

Gene and I made yesterday and the ones we'll make today are all covered in his mercy—even if we made some mistakes. The sun rises every day—and with it comes new hope!

Have we prayed together about the decisions we need to make?

Sometimes Gene and I need to be reminded that because we have a personal relationship with the King of Kings, we can confidently seek his guidance through prayer. "Let us therefore come boldly to the throne of grace, that we may obtain mercy and find grace to help in time of need" (Heb. 4:16 NKJV). As you pray, ask the Holy Spirit to reveal to you the next right choice. After all, one of his roles is to be our guide.

Do we believe God can make a way when our situation looks impossible?

Steve was drafted and served his country in Vietnam. He married Rosie six weeks after he returned home. The year overseas profoundly impacted Steve, and Rosie couldn't understand why he had come home so different. Post-Traumatic Stress Disorder—PTSD—wasn't even a "thing" yet, but it still triggered wild emotions for Steve and made him confused about who he was and how he should relate to those around him.

Steve was proud of his military service but believed he would look weak if he opened up about the complicated internal struggles he was experiencing. This sometimes led to arguments and serious strain on their marriage. Isaiah 43:19 was a comfort: "See, I am doing a new thing! Now it springs up; do you not perceive it? I am making a way in the wilderness and streams in the wasteland." Believing that divorce was not an option, they both made the next right choice and sought counseling. Later, Steve joined a support group. They had some rough years, but they learned many things, and they're now putting those lessons to work through Point Man Ministries,[3] connecting hurting veterans and their families with others who have successfully transitioned home after war. Steve and Rosie will soon celebrate their fiftieth wedding anniversary.

Have we read the Bible together and looked for God's direction?

One of the hardest things for Gene and me is to try to find time to read the Bible together every day. Our schedules are busy. We're distracted by work. We live in "hurry-up" mode, and taking even a few minutes to read God's Word together is challenging. But check out the reward for doing that: "The LORD says, 'I will guide you along the best pathway for your life. I will advise you and watch over you'" (Ps. 32:8 NLT). I think that means that if we make the time to read his Word, we'll get wisdom for making our next right choice.

Of One Mind

In my first marriage, I (Cindy) struggled for many years with infertility. About three years into the struggle to conceive and carry the baby to term, one decision that my husband and I had to face was, "If our efforts at having a child don't result in us becoming parents, at what point will we consider adoption?" It was a huge decision, and much hung on it—how much medical intervention we would endure, for instance, and for how long. There were so many factors to consider, and for about a year the question haunted us. *Should we keep trying month after month? Should we take another step in infertility treatments? Should we cease our extraordinary efforts and just wait on the Lord, learning to be content as a childless couple?*

We wanted to follow the Lord's leading, but our desire to become parents was so powerful—how would we ever know that it was "time" to make one decision or the other? Finally, we arrived at a pre-decision: We valued unity in our marriage. Therefore, we would wait on the Lord until we were both of the *same mind* before we would change our direction. We would trust God that if the time was right to consider greater medical intervention, we'd both feel that way at the same time, and if it was time to consider adoption, we would both be led by God in that direction at the same time.

At times one or the other of us was interested in pursuing adoption, but never both at the same time. Thanks to our pre-decision, our course of action was clear—we would not pursue it because we were not of the same mind. We also discovered something: neither of us felt that in vitro fertilization was for us.

A decade passed, and during that time we experienced a heartbreaking miscarriage. We also charted ovulations and tried various medications.

Finally, both of us were interested at the same time in pursuing adoption. We began a six-month investigation into adoption alternatives. During that process, we saw that any healthy newborn had a long list of parents ready and eager to adopt it, but there were older children with tough stories waiting for and hoping for parents. Both of us were drawn to adopting an older at-risk child.

Eleven years into our marriage, we adopted a nine-year-old boy—our son, Ben. We knew the timing was God's and that Ben was meant to be ours! The pre-decision to honor the unity of our marriage by seeking God's will together, waiting until we were both of the same mind, was how we approached this major decision, and it served us very well.

Just Enough Light

All this talk about making the next right choice reminds me (Carol) of all the time I've spent in my life thinking about and trying to find God's will for me. Maybe you've done the same. There have certainly been enough books written and sermons preached about finding God's will to show that for many people that search is a major source of uncertainty and yearning.

As a university student, I was obsessed with discovering the specific and perfect will of God whenever I faced major decisions—like whom to marry, where to live, and what I should do with the rest of my life. But I doubted that he cared as much about the small decisions. That turned me into a person who was always jumping from what I believed was the precise center of God's will to my perception of the next perfect choice. It was exhausting.

As time went on, I came to understand that where I am right at this moment (or any other) is the "growing point" where God wants to be at work in my life. He has given me a mind, his Word, and the Holy Spirit as my guide, and when I ask for wisdom, he gives it liberally. James 1:5–6 (NLT) says: "If you need wisdom, ask our generous God, and he will give it to you. He will not rebuke you for asking. But when you ask him, be sure that your faith is in God alone."

The fact that you picked up this book tells me something about you. You and your spouse are in a situation that, at least at present, lacks resolution. You're making multiple difficult decisions every day, and it's easy to second-guess yourself and wonder if you made the right choice. *What else might I have done? What else* should *I have done?*

Consider Psalm 119:105 (NKJV): "Your word is a lamp to my feet and a light to my path." When we live in a crisis that doesn't end, we need to look for just enough light to make the next right choice—even if we can't see far enough to guess at the choice after that. He has promised to provide—if we ask—the wisdom to make that next step.

As a couple, commit to trusting the one who sees your end from the beginning. "Trust in the LORD with all your heart; do not depend on your own understanding. Seek his will in all you do, and he will show you which path to take" (Prov. 3:5–6 NLT). J. Randall O'Brien wrote, "We walk by faith, not sight, or we go no farther. Yet, a voice calls us forward. . . . Perhaps there is something better than understanding God after all—trusting him."[4]

Remember the 10-Second Rule that you read at the beginning of this chapter? "Just do the next thing you're reasonably certain Jesus wants you to do. (And commit to it immediately—in the next ten seconds—before you change your mind!)" What good advice—even, or perhaps especially, when you find life and your family in crisis. God will illuminate the next step. And when you feel an alertness in your mind and a stirring in your heart, you can know that it's the Holy Spirit nudging you to make the next right choice—soon!

Will all your decisions be perfect? Will your next choice change the difficulty of your current circumstances? Probably not. But if you follow the advice in this chapter, you'll be seeking wisdom from wise people, spending time in prayer and in the Word of God, listening to the needs of your spouse, and coming up with your own list of "Pre-decisions We're Committed to in Our Marriage." And armed with those resources, you'll find yourself making the next right choice.

Discussion Questions
for Couples and Small Groups

1. What one concept in this chapter most challenged your thinking?
2. Discuss the 10-Second Rule itself: *Just do the next thing you're reasonably certain Jesus wants you to do. (And commit to it immediately—in the next ten seconds—before you change your mind!)* When in your life have you felt a prompting from God and acted on it immediately to do something tangible to meet someone else's need? What happened?
3. Name a time in your marriage when you and your spouse were not of one mind about an important decision. How did you decide, and how did it turn out?
4. Of all the pre-decisions listed on pages 45–47, are there any that you liked well enough to adopt in your own marriage?
5. The chapter quotes Proverbs 19:20 (NLT): "Get all the advice and instruction you can, so you will be wise the rest of your life." Do you find it difficult to ask for advice? Why? Do you and your spouse feel the same or differently about this? Share an example.

CHAPTER 3

Anger Is Not the Enemy

People who fly into a rage always make a bad landing.

—Will Rogers

When you noticed in the table of contents that this book contained a chapter on anger, you probably thought something like, *Okay, yeah—guilty as charged. I know I need to control my temper a little better. That's what you're going to tell me, right—that every time I blow up, I set our marriage back like a hundred years?*

Actually, that's just half of it. As destructive and difficult and downright dangerous as anger can be (as in the story you're about to read), it's also true that anger can be put to positive use.

Still, if you're feeling guilty about your most recent display of temper and see anger as primarily destructive, you're not alone. And there's good reason for thinking so. In some places in the Bible, anger is condemned (Eccles. 7:9 and Matt.

5:22) and called one of the "works of the flesh" (Gal. 5:19–20 ESV). It's linked with pride, arrogance, and insolence (Prov. 21:24), cruelty (Gen. 49:7), malice, slander, and filthy language (Col. 3:8), and the list goes on. In Colossians 3:8, we're instructed to rid ourselves of anger and rage. And there's a long list of biblical characters whose anger is considered sinful: Cain, Esau, Balaam, Saul, Ahab, Jonah, and many more.

On the other hand, Ephesians 4:26 (NASB) says, "Be angry, and *yet* do not sin; do not let the sun go down on your anger." So it seems that one can be angry without sinning. Clearly, anger is a complex subject.

Our interest in anger in this chapter is in how it makes better—or worse—your and your spouse's attempts to respond to the crises and threats that push their way into your life.

The Mug and the Refrigerator

"And another thing!" my friend Margie shouted. Her husband, Rico, stood across the kitchen from her, like two boxers in opposite corners, waiting for the bell, eyeing each other for possible weaknesses.

Their marriage had never been an easy or a tranquil one. It wasn't that they didn't love each other. It was a second marriage for both of them and both had kids from their first marriages—those things in themselves will create tensions and disagreements, as Cindy and I (Dave) well know. In Margie and Rico's case, those tensions were exacerbated by the fact that both of them were recovering alcoholics and in many ways still thought like addicts, as recovering addicts tend to do, which is why they need AA. And Margie and Rico were both faithful in attending their meetings, as well as church. Margie in particular threw herself into her faith as she once had into the party life, leaving her radio tuned all day to a local Christian station that played praise music, to which she sang along. Those things *helped* keep their minds and emotions straight. *Helped.* But too often, the old attitudes crept back, and when that happened, they sometimes came to the surface in arguments like this one. And this one had erupted, once again, over a conflict about the kids—Rico's adult son from his previous marriage, Rico Junior, had been kicked out by his mother. He needed a place to live. He had shown up late the night before with a backpack, his guitar, and a garbage bag full of dirty clothes.

This time, Rico crossed the line first. Frustrated at Margie's knee-jerk anger, at the increased frequency, or so it seemed to him, of these arguments, and at his own frustration about what to do about his son, who should be able to support himself but apparently couldn't, he said, "You know what? I liked you better when you were drinking."

Flabbergasted, hardly believing what she'd just heard, Margie crossed the line next. She cocked her arm and threw her mostly full coffee mug, with all her might, right at Rico.

It would have missed him by a good foot and a half, except that Rico was standing right in front of the refrigerator and the mug she was throwing was a favorite of his, a souvenir from a fishing trip to Florida he'd taken with his buddies. Ignoring the coffee that showered him, he reached for the mug to save it but managed only to get a couple of his fingers in the way. The mug hit the solid handle of the refrigerator door and shattered just as Rico tried to close his hand around it. What he closed his hand around, with speed and force, were the sharp edges of the broken mug, which sliced into his skin. Blood spurted.

Instantly remorseful and feeling completely at fault (even though the argument had been mutual), Margie wished she could rush to him, wrap a towel around his bleeding hand, and doctor it for him—but the anger and accusation in his eyes kept her feet firmly planted. He grabbed a dish towel from the rack, gave her one last heated glance over his shoulder, and headed into the bathroom to clean and bandage his wound.

For Margie and Rico, even though arguments and bursts of anger were far from rare, they had never ended in bloodshed or injury. They usually erupted in words and ended in sullen silence, followed eventually by apologies and reconciliation. As this one would—they were, after all, committed to each other and to their marriage and forgiving once the tide of anger had passed, and both realized that they brought as many skeletons and bad habits into their marriage as their partner did.

And yet . . .

They knew this would not be their last heated argument. They just hoped it would be the last one to draw blood or result in bandages.

Anger Management

We humans are so variable in how we feel and express and use anger, aren't we? Some people get angry at the drop of a hat—or the raising of an eyebrow, or a lack of eye contact, or a reply deemed too curt or flippant. Or crumbs left on the counter or a lack of ability to master the myriad tiny buttons on the six different remotes sitting in front of the entertainment center. Or spending money on eating out ten times in a single week or insisting on watching football every Sunday afternoon *and* Sunday night *and* Thursday night throughout the interminable football season. Or the call that comes in from your parents and/or siblings for an hour or so every day, usually right at dinnertime. Or insisting on putting a check in the offering plate every Sunday, rain or shine, even when you're behind in paying the bills, or, or, or . . . Research tells us that as much as 20 percent of the population has a hard time controlling their anger.[1]

Others seem to never get angry. You can insult them, cheat them, defraud them, yell at them, give them the cold shoulder, poke 'em, prod 'em, kick 'em, stick 'em, and they'll just give you the benefit of the doubt and try to make things right with you. People like that make me so angry . . .

Whatever your own habits and inclinations are regarding the emotion of anger, you can find examples in Scripture that reflect it, besides those I mentioned earlier. It's easy to conclude from James 1:19–20—"Everyone should be quick to listen, slow to speak and slow to become angry, because human anger does not produce the righteousness that God desires"—that anger is something to be guarded against, and that we'd all be better off avoiding. Remember in Numbers 20:10–12 when Moses got mad and struck the rock with his staff to make the water gush forth—and as a result God refused to let him set foot in the promised land? Or when Cain got mad at his brother Abel in Genesis 4:3–8 and murdered him?

On the other hand, it was Jesus who got angry enough with the money changers in the temple in John 2:13–17 to make himself a whip (premeditation!) and use it to drive the money changers out of the temple courtyard and overturn their tables. In that passage and in similar passages in Matthew, Mark, and Luke, the Bible doesn't say that Jesus was angry—it just tells us what he did. But given the number of passages in Scripture that talk about the wrath of God, I think we can assume that Jesus, as God the Son, must be capable of anger as well. Of course, his actions in the temple may have been intended to chasten, for their own good, those who were profiting from worship. But does that mean he wasn't angry at the same time? Did you ever get mad at your child for starting to run out into the street in front of a truck? I rest my case.

If Jesus is to be our example in all things, then doesn't that mean that there's some justification for chasing out whoever the money changers are in our own temple, and if it takes some anger to motivate and empower us to chase them, well then . . .

Theologians tell us that the difference between the wrath of God and the anger of man is that God's wrath is always both holy and justified. About the most we can say of our own anger is that it often *feels* justified—at the time. Yet how often after you've allowed yourself a glorious bout of screaming and foot stomping have you calmed down and, maybe a day or two later, felt a great deal of remorse over what you now realize was the totally unjust way you dragged over the coals someone you love very much and hate to hurt?

The Positive Uses of Anger

Let's take the positive side of anger first.

And yes, you're right, there was a time I probably wouldn't have thought that sentence made much sense. *Positive* side of anger? Isn't anger always destructive?

I think it's fair to say that anger always *risks* being destructive. But when it descends on us, are there ways we can use anger for positive results? Yes.

Anger can provide motivation.

Some of us already know from personal experience that when you're angry—or when someone you love is angry—you find extra energy and determination to push on toward a goal.

Anger can actually benefit your marriage.

Says PsyBlog: "The problem is that when you hide your anger, your partner doesn't know they've done something wrong. And so they keep doing it. And that doesn't do your relationship any good."[2]

Anger teaches you something about yourself.

Studies have shown that getting angry can demonstrate to us (after we've cooled off, most likely) truths about ourselves. Our faults, perhaps—but also what things we care about enough to get mad. And those truths help us see ways in which we can improve our lives as well as our marriage.

Anger reduces violence. Wait—what?

Yeah, it's true, actually. Our mental image of violent encounters—a bar brawl, for instance—usually includes two people getting so angry at each other that they lose control and violence ensues. And yes, that can happen. But often, when one person gets angry, the other looks for ways to de-escalate the situation. Anger provides a strong social signal to which people respond.

Let's go back to Margie and Rico. Once Margie had apologized for her outburst and for breaking Rico's favorite mug and cutting his hand, and once he'd commiserated with Margie for the disruption of their lives brought about by the sudden, unannounced arrival of his son, they were motivated to find ways to discuss the difficult situation as calmly as possible and work together toward a solution. After all, Rico loved and trusted Margie enough to know that even though she did tend toward volatility in her emotions, both positively and negatively, it was also true that she was a wellspring of love and compassion, and if she was *that angry* about the situation—well, Rico could see her point. This would massively impact her life.

In their case, Rico Junior ended up staying with them for many months. It wasn't ideal for any of them. But Margie, once she was rational again, could see that pressing her husband to kick his beloved-if-irresponsible son out would likely make him resent her for it. Better to suck it up and live with it until a better option could be found. They might have come to that solution anyway, but understanding the depths of their mutual anger helped them get there.

Anger can be a catalyst for communication.

When my (Dave's) kids were tiny, they would often climb up into my lap for some "Dad time." The only problem was, Dad wasn't always fully engaged. Dad might have been working on an article or a story or paying bills. So as my son or daughter talked to me, my mind (and eyes) might have been elsewhere.

Not something kids would be likely to miss, even if we try to fool them with little bits of pseudo-dialogue like, "Uh-huh. Yeah, I know. Wow, that's really something." One of my daughters in particular, Sarah, would take that type of parental neglect for only so long before she took action—and in her case, "action" meant that she would put her hands one on either side of my face, turn my face toward her, and when she had eye contact, move ahead with her monologue without losing a beat. And it worked. I paid attention at that point because I could see and hear and feel that this was an important moment for her.

When we see the anger on our spouse's face and hear it in their voice, our reaction is somewhat the same—we're likely to tune in even if we've been only half paying attention up to that point. (And our lack of attention may have been what sparked the anger in the first place.)

But—what would happen if you began to suspect that your spouse's anger to get your attention was only feigned or self-indulgent? That they just didn't like being ignored and had discovered that an angry tone, a bit more volume, and a wrinkled brow got your attention? You would probably get angry! The truth is, in *any* of these positive uses of anger, it doesn't work all the time and isn't likely to work well unless we deliberately choose to work with God through our anger.

Keep in mind that letting yourself descend into anger and dwell there isn't good for you regardless of what effect it has on your marriage. Anger and stress are closely related, and too much anger, like too much stress, can affect such things as your immune system, making it less effective. Too much anger and stress can promote the creation of more stomach acid, cause bronchial congestion, and other things. Occasional anger, if channeled in the right direction and not directed against your spouse, can be helpful. Too much anger, regardless of where it's channeled, can hurt you.

Anger can be a tool. But it's always—always—a dangerous and risky one.

The Dangers of Anger and How to Avoid Them

An article on the *Psychology Today* website links two other characteristics with anger: *resentment* and *contempt*. And to balance the scale, it places opposite them: *compassion* and *empathy*.[3] You don't have to think too long or too hard to form an opinion about which marriage stands a better chance of continuing in good health—the one characterized by anger, resentment, and contempt or the one characterized by compassion and empathy.

Given that anger is an emotion most of us are unable to avoid feeling on at least infrequent occasions, and given that it can, when given free rein, do a lot of damage to a relationship, especially one already struggling with unpleasant circumstances, we would be wise to remind ourselves of the techniques for reducing the effects of anger, whether our own or our spouse's, on our marriage.

What are some of these negative effects of anger?

- It damages the feelings of safety and trust on which your marriage depends.

- It damages self-esteem by causing guilt and shame in both the angry spouse and the spouse who is the object of the anger.
- It makes us fearful and reluctant to give of ourselves and to receive what our spouse offers.
- It can cause or increase feelings of distance between you and your spouse.
- It leads to loneliness, sadness, and anxiety.
- It can increase the temptation for us to "act out" in whatever ways most tempt us in response to the anger we feel was unjustified.
- It not only hurts us, it increases our fear of being hurt in the future.
- It can increase the symptoms of depression—perhaps as much as tenfold. This is true not only of the angry spouse but also of the spouse who is the object of the anger.

You probably already have your favorite techniques for dealing with anger in your marriage, and some of them may be listed below. See if you can find additional "new favorites" here.

Don't hesitate to use the old tried-and-true methods for handling anger.

Do this even if both you and your spouse know them well and understand exactly what you're doing. In a dangerous moment, sometimes a familiar approach is the one that can defuse the situation best.

- *Use "I" statements, not "you" statements.* Rather than saying, "You always do this! I ask a question that's important to me and you completely ignore me!" say, "It makes me feel unvalued and ignored when I ask a question and you don't respond."
- *Count to ten before speaking.* Pretty old advice, right? When you were a kid, your mom probably told you to do this before getting into an argument or a fight. But as one of my friends used to say, "The reason clichés are clichés is because they're usually true." And this technique, as elementary as it is, works. It gives you a chance to choose your words carefully and to cool down.
- *Practice active listening.* We all know how active listening works, and we've probably used it ourselves or noticed when someone else is using it with us: you simply find an unobtrusive way of repeating back what you just heard. That shows that you heard and understood, and it also affirms your spouse's feelings.
- *Touch.* Hold a hand. Stroke an arm. Hug. If it's appropriate and mutual, try some intimacy. But be sensitive—some people find that touch helps them bridge the gap created by anger, but others feel manipulated and resentful if touch comes before their feelings have been healed.

Remind yourself of biblical attitudes toward anger.

Besides those passages already mentioned in this chapter, there are a number of other biblical passages about anger, including:

- Psalm 37:8—don't let your anger prod you into sin
- Proverbs 15:1—gentleness pacifies anger
- Proverbs 19:19—anger brings its own punishment
- Proverbs 29:8—anger may be averted by wisdom

Probably the biggest take-away of these and other verses about anger: anger is clearly powerful and dangerous, or else the verses addressing it wouldn't be filled with words of caution. In your marriage, as in the rest of your life: handle with care.

Don't let the sun go down on your anger.

Make every attempt to respond to any rift in your relationship caused by anger in a way that is Christlike, biblical, and completed by the end of the day. As Roy Milam of Cornerstone Marriage and Family Ministries says, "Prolonged anger hurts deeply and destroys marital harmony, perhaps as much as an act of infidelity."[4]

When anger rears its head, both of you need to proceed with patience.

This, perhaps, is why James tells us to be slow to speak and slow to become angry. Patience! It enables you to be more objective (anger is, after all, the most subjective of emotions), more introspective, more honest, and more effective. There's no rush. Take a deep breath. Patience. Anger by its very nature feels urgent, but when you as a couple are already facing another crisis, it is especially important to be patient with your own and your spouse's anger.

Cindy found this to be true when she and I both came face-to-face with our own anger and each other's. I'll let her tell the story.

Cindy's Anger Dilemma

Dave and I (Cindy) had a particularly trying year in 2009. Dave, after suffering for years from a serious medical condition, was advised to have two major surgeries four months apart—surgeries known for their likely complications. Unfortunately, he experienced every complication in the book and probably invented new ones. He was in and out of the hospital fourteen times during that calendar year, sometimes just for a few hours on IVs, sometimes overnight or for a few days, and sometimes for a week or more, twice in ICU.

We made a great team dealing with it all but for two exceptions, and both of those involved anger.

The first issue surfaced during Dave's initial hospitalization, when we discovered that we had vastly different styles of communication with the medical personnel. Dave is a quiet sufferer. No surprise there, as Dave is a quiet man. However, in my opinion he wasn't communicating enough to the doctors and nurses about his symptoms. His answers to their questions, it seemed to me, were minimizing the problems he was experiencing, and what they weren't asking he wasn't telling.

I, on the other hand, am very verbal with medical personnel and am not shy about making sure I'm getting answers to my questions. So what did I do? I spoke up *for* him, to the point where at times the doctor and I, on opposite sides of the bed, were discussing Dave back and forth in third person as he lay silently between us, as if he weren't even there. I was a bit dense at first, not realizing that this irritated him. Then I caught "the look" and knew I'd crossed a line.

"I can speak for myself, you know," he told me when the doctor had gone. "How about if you let me do the communicating? After all, it is my body. I'm the only one who knows what I'm experiencing."

I got the point and tried biting my lip the next few times a doctor was in the room, but it was hard. Sometimes I'd remain quiet for a bit, then feel compelled to add some information. Clearly, this irritated Dave, and his irritation irritated me! Couldn't he see I was only trying to help? And why wasn't he saying more and asking more when the doctor or nurse was present?

Dave and I are both peacemakers at heart. We seldom have to deal with anger between us, and we certainly weren't used to a recurring unresolved tension. Usually, we address our issues head-on and get them resolved fairly easily, but with each return to the hospital we found ourselves doing an uneasy dance around this communication issue. Either I'd feel angry with him for not communicating sufficiently (in my estimation) or he'd feel angry with me for taking over the conversation. It took several hospitalizations for me to learn to hold my tongue until the end of each doctor's visit. Then, if I felt something important needed to be addressed, I'd pose it as a question for Dave, but we could both tell we had some unresolved anger over the issue.

Each time Dave was discharged we would hope it was for good. Instead, for months, rather than growing stronger, Dave remained weak and his symptoms problematic. It soon became clear that, among other issues, his body was having trouble staying hydrated; when he became too dehydrated we'd need to go to the hospital for him to get IV fluids.

And that led to our second struggle with anger one evening when Dave's symptoms of dehydration seemed to me unusually intense. His voice was weak and raspy, his walk was a shuffle, he got winded just moving from the couch to the kitchen, and his color was poor.

"Dave," I said reluctantly, "I know you don't want to make another trip to the hospital, but I really believe you need an IV treatment again."

"I'll double up on the Gatorade," he answered. "I can get past this without going to the hospital. I've done it before." Dave is soft-spoken and exceedingly patient, but when his mind is made up, there is a certain quiet firmness in his voice. I knew I shouldn't push him or I'd frustrate him, so I dropped it.

A few hours went by and he seemed worse to me. Hesitantly, I said, "I'm not sure you're seeing your symptoms the way I am. I think you need an IV. Let's go to the hospital."

"I know how I feel," Dave replied, his eyes meeting mine. "Let me decide when I need to go to the hospital. I'll keep up with the fluids and feel better by morning."

I was worried about him and frustrated that he wouldn't take my advice, but again, not wanting to anger him, I didn't push the point. A short time later we climbed into bed. I wanted to make one more appeal but kept my thoughts and feelings to myself. Then I felt him trembling.

"Dave, do you realize you're shaking? Please hear me—we need to get you into the hospital."

"Cindy," he said, his weak voice laced with frustration, "no."

Now I was scared and angry. Scared that if I stopped pushing he'd become critically ill. Angry at this illness and how it was ravaging my husband's body. Angry at myself for not persuading him into the hospital sooner. Angry at him for his stubborn refusal to get the help I was sure he needed. As I lay by his side praying for wisdom and help, the whole bed started to shake from his trembling. I sat up and turned on the light. I knew beyond a doubt that I had to intervene. But how? Should I just dial 911 against his wishes? Should I plead? Insist? Yell?

"The entire bed is shaking, Dave. This is beyond anything you've experienced. You know we have no choice."

Finally, I saw resignation in his face. He threw off the covers. I hurriedly got dressed and off we went to the hospital.

Dave wound up in the ICU that night in renal failure. I stood by as doctors and nurses worked on him, a host of emotions flooding me: relief that he was in good hands. Fear for his safety. Desperation. Fatigue. And to my surprise, I had a heart full of anger toward my husband, and even more at myself for allowing the peacekeeper side of me to keep me from insisting on getting Dave to the hospital sooner. I'd known the "right" thing to do, but I hadn't done it for fear of angering the man I loved. This was a complex anger I didn't know how to handle. *Surely,* I reasoned, *my anger will pass. It's just a symptom of my lack of control over all these circumstances.*

As Dave recovered over the next several days, the sharpness of my anger faded, but I had to face the fact that it was still there, a red flag that something was wrong—something we would need to address together. However, the last thing my husband needed was any emotional baggage from me while he was so ill. So I kept it between God and myself. I poured out my anger in prayer and decided that at the right time in the future, when Dave was in far better health, I'd need to bring it up even if it meant having a difficult conversation.

I was fortunate that God had already used some earlier life trials to teach me a few things about anger. I thought through and affirmed each of those things:

- The initial surge of anger is an emotion that happens *to* us. *Feeling* anger isn't a sin, but the *choices* we make when we are angry could lead to sin if we aren't careful and thoughtful.
- Anger presents us with choices. Will we choose to feed it or defuse it? Will we choose to rant or resolve?
- The moment we feel anger, we need to slow down rather than blow up.
- Anger is often the result of unmet expectations. We need to allow anger to be a tool—a signal that it's time to discern the reason behind our anger and solve that problem.
- Discerning takes time, and that's good because it allows our anger to cool.

With those beliefs in place and lots of time sitting by a hospital bed to think and pray, I came to some conclusions.

What unmet expectations did I have? I expected that Dave would have respect for my perspective when it came to medical issues. I expected that if either of us was facing a medical crisis, we'd be "in it together" and not disregard the strong feelings of the other.

And that's when it dawned on me—my "overbearing" communication style in the hospital was angering Dave for the same reason. I was not showing respect for his perspective when it came to communicating with doctors. I was disrespecting him and I needed to stop it, even if it meant biting my tongue. However, I determined, in a crisis when I believed his well-being was at stake, I would speak up.

Over a month later, when Dave was feeling better, we finally did have that difficult conversation. Fortunately, it didn't turn out to be nearly as difficult as I had anticipated. I began by explaining that I wanted to show him respect by not taking over the dialogue between him and his doctors and nurses, and not speaking about him to the doctors and nurses as if he wasn't even in the room. I wanted to learn to be patient in allowing Dave to communicate in his own way and his own time with medical personnel. I apologized for what I'd done and asked his forgiveness, which he freely and tenderly gave.

Then I explained that I also wanted his respect for my perspective, especially in what I considered to be a medical crisis. I assured him that I would never again sit idly by if I believed he was in danger. I loved him too much to do so and would rather risk his wrath than his life. Dave assured me that he heard me and appreciated that love. Talking it through, each of us expressing our thoughts and feelings and each of us affirming that we understood and respected what the other was saying, defused the anger we'd both been struggling with. As the year went on and Dave required more hospitalizations, we had ample opportunity to practice our improved respect for one another.

We've faced a few other health challenges since that horrific year, but we've never again had to face anger because of them. We laugh today that in medical situations I have a tendency to over-communicate while Dave has a tendency to under-communicate, but we figure that as partners in our health care, between the two of us it all balances out.

Perhaps my biggest take-away from the entire experience is that although the anger came uninvited and was unpleasant to feel, when given to God it became a tool that taught me about myself, was a catalyst for communication, and gave me the motivation to pursue an important and eye-opening conversation. The experience taught me that I don't need to fear anger, nor do I need to fall victim to it. May you, too, invite God to use your anger to his good purposes.

Discussion Questions *for* Couples and Small Groups

1. What change do you want to make after reading this chapter?
2. Consider this quote, often attributed to Groucho Marx: "Speak when you are angry—and you'll make the best speech you'll ever regret." Describe a time in your marriage when you spoke in anger and lived to regret it.
3. Who in your life, if anyone, has modeled for you the truth of James 1:19–20: "Everyone should be quick to listen, slow to speak and slow to become angry, because human anger does not produce the righteousness that God desires"? How has their example influenced your behavior?
4. Which of the methods for handling anger listed on pages 69–71 are the most helpful for you? Is there another method you can suggest?

CHAPTER 4

Forgive Freely

> Forgiveness usually isn't a one-time experience. It's an ongoing process. You have to work at it.
>
> —Elisa Morgan

Regarding the power of forgiveness, I (Gene) often think about couples Carol and I have met who survived major blows to their marriage: betrayal, affairs, or addiction to pornography. If a marriage can withstand that kind of assault and remain intact, then deep forgiveness must have been given and received. And you don't have to look far for confirmation that forgiveness is an important topic—just Google "books on forgiveness."[1] We've all seen way too many couples wind up in divorce court due to their inability to move beyond such serious issues as betrayal and infidelity.

But that's not what this chapter is about. This book deals with the blows that hit a reasonably happy couple from the *outside*, rather than the *inside*. As Carol and I dealt with the arrest, trial, and conviction of our son for a serious crime, there were times when our tempers flared, patience grew thin, unkind words were spoken, anger mounted, or we reverted to the silent treatment. We still loved each other deeply, and we both knew it, but there have been many times on this ongoing, ceaselessly stressful journey when we realized that our behavior or our words had been less than ideal, when we had not in fact treated each other in the way that we wanted to be treated ourselves, and we needed to say, "Will you forgive me?" or "I'm sorry." If a marriage has staying power, then forgiveness of necessity must be a major part of the glue that holds that relationship together. It's essential not just to being able to cope with everyday living but also to finding comforting closeness as a couple in the middle of chaos.

Dan and Leigh's Story

Leigh writes:

> At seventeen, our only son, Luke—strong and athletic, generous with his time, a good student, loyal to his friends, and a leader in school and in church with a heart for Jesus—got his driver's license. He showed me his license and said, "Look, Mom, I'm an organ donor."
>
> I put dinner on hold; we sat down to discuss his decision. Luke knew that when I was five years old, bone had been transplanted into my right femur because of a tumor. Luke also had a close friend whose father suffered with a genetic

kidney disease and had to have a transplant, and who might one day need a transplant herself because of that disease. "If something should ever happen to me," Luke said, "I want my organs to help others. And after the doctors have taken everything they can use, I want to be cremated." Seeing the tears in my eyes, he said in his unique, lighthearted way, "Aww, Mom, could you imagine the land space this body would cover?" He was at that age six feet, four inches tall and weighed 240 pounds.

Luke's seventeenth year was busy. He played his favorite sport as part of the Washington Junior Golf Association. Dan was able to be with him at many of his tournaments, and the two of them played the game together weekly. One day Luke said, "Mom, I want to take you to lunch this Saturday. I'm buying. Life is getting busy, and we need this time together."

That Saturday, over a lunch of fish and chips, we talked. He had been filling out college applications, and a few schools had offered golf scholarships. "But what do you want to do for the rest of your life?" I asked.

"Mom, I've prayed about that and I just don't know. One thing I do feel is that I will be very far away."

Tears gathered in my eyes again, thinking about the colleges on his list that were most of the way across the country. He grabbed my hand and said, "Mama, no matter how far away I am, we are always connected at the heart."

In July, he went to leadership camp and was busy preparing for a big golf tournament at which coaches from several colleges would be checking him out. At one of the tournaments his score broke a Washington Junior Golf Association record, and that news hit the local newspaper the Friday he returned home. On Sunday, the whole family was coming over for dinner—our daughter Marisa, son-in-law Jason, Luke, Dan, and me. Luke had been out shopping for clothes, and he returned later than he'd expected. "I really need some practice time at the golf course," he told me. "Can you hold dinner so I can get an hour in?" I was a bit annoyed, but I agreed. I let him borrow my car, since his clunker was low on gas.

Minutes later, we heard sirens. Then we got a call from Luke's phone but from someone we didn't know, telling us there had been a horrible car accident. Dan rushed out the door, calling back over his shoulder for me to stay at home, pray, and call Marisa and Jason while he went to the scene. When he got there, the EMTs were preparing to airlift Luke to Harborview Medical Center, the major trauma center in Seattle. Dan called and asked me to come to the scene, explaining that a police escort was going to take us to Harborview.

When I got to the scene, my car had been totally smashed in from the passenger side to the driver's side; the other car was a Suburban. I saw Luke's shoes and a great deal of blood, and I fell on my knees and began to cry and pray. Two chaplains drove us to Harborview. Dan was quiet on the way; it felt to me as if he was shutting down. My mind was racing, and I just wanted to get to my boy.

At Harborview, we were told that the injuries Luke had sustained were critical. He had a severe closed-head injury and extensive damage to his lungs. When he came out of his long surgery, we were allowed to see him. He was on full life support with a probe sticking out of his head, but otherwise he looked as handsome as ever, as if he were just sleeping in a bed much too small for him, with his large feet sticking out from under the blankets. I sat with him and prayed. Dan walked in and out, not saying much to anyone. Our pastor said he was concerned about Dan, but I was too wrapped up in my own grief to be able to offer Dan any support.

I sat with Luke all night. I didn't know how much he could hear or understand, but I talked, telling him how much I loved him. I held his big warm hand and touched his soft cheek.

The pressure in his brain kept increasing. Dan called me out of the room—someone from LifeCenter Northwest was there and asked us about organ donation. Even though Luke and I had had an earlier, very detailed conversation about this, my heart rebelled.

Dan said quietly, "Honey, isn't this something Luke wanted?"

Our pastor asked us to come into Luke's room and pray. During that prayer, the Holy Spirit nudged me, and as clearly as if Luke were speaking to me from the other side of the room, I heard my son say, "Mom, I just want to help people."

I looked at Dan and, tears blinding my eyes, slightly nodded my yes. He nodded back, and we left the room to sign papers.

All of us in the family were allowed time to say our goodbyes to Luke. For a while, I sat with Luke by myself and told him again how much I loved him. Then I said, "Honey, it's okay for you to go to be with Jesus. It's okay. We will always be connected at the heart."

Grieving Differently

For Dan and Leigh, the accident and Luke's death triggered unanticipated stress on their marriage:

We returned home to a discarded salmon dinner sitting on the stove. Dan hardly said a word. I was reeling. I wanted to scream, yell, or punch something. I was mad at God. How could he do this to us? Dan and I went to bed together, but we were very separate in our grief. Dan was quiet, shut down, and I was filled with emotion and wanted to scream and cry. I felt so much anger at God—as well as at Dan for shutting down just when I needed him to engage.

I awoke in the night and began screaming into my pillow. I wanted the pain to stop. I wanted comfort. Dan was on his own broken, grief-ridden journey, and we were no help to each other.

It was a long, dysfunctional journey for both Dan and me to get to a place of grace. We first had to walk the long, broken road of misunderstanding, unforgiveness, bitterness, and resentments. Unfortunately, both of us went to the wrong things for comfort. I ran to food and overspending. Dan ran to gambling and alcohol. We fought countless arguments, pointing fingers and casting blame. I spent many nights alone while Dan was off escaping his pain in ways that ultimately can't possibly satisfy.

For my part, I would overeat and lie prostrate on the floor, crying out my misery and asking Jesus to take me home. I felt done in. Alone. Afraid. Dan was in his own prison of misery. We moved to separate bedrooms. Every time Dan would drink and gamble, he came home sorry, repentant, and asking for forgiveness, but I showed him no mercy. I was still wrapped up in my own bitterness and pain.

A friend invited me to GriefShare,[2] and slowly I began unpeeling the layers of my emotional brokenness. My prayers changed from repetitive *whys* to "Show me your hand, oh Lord." Over time I began to submit to the healing grace and forgiveness our compassionate Lord provides. And things began to shift.

Forgiveness Issues

Archibald Hart wrote, "Forgiveness is surrendering my right to hurt you for hurting me."[3] In marriage, hurt often involves closing down and building walls of resentment and unforgiveness when our spouse responds to a crisis differently than we do. Forgiveness requires giving up the resentment we feel for the omission or commission of something that hurts us. For married people, this is more challenging when you're married to someone who doesn't seem to get why you can't get over the pain you feel in response to a situation you never wanted and didn't anticipate. Resentment can also arise when a couple experiences different modes of grieving. If you and your spouse have dissimilar ways of expressing your sorrow, one or both of you may assume that the other doesn't care about what happened as much as you do. But grief is not a competition in strength or endurance or volume.

When life hands us an unwanted surprise or unexpected challenge, it's easy to point the finger at our spouse and find a reason to blame the person we're closest to for not being involved enough, for not being caring and compassionate enough toward us, for not understanding our pain, or for running away (emotionally or physically). Our emotions get in the way. We sometimes hold grudges for long periods of time. Sometimes those negative responses can be traced back to personality differences between us and our spouse; at other times we respond negatively because we feel misunderstood. Sometimes we feel like the one most negatively impacted by the circumstances while our partner gets engrossed in work or other activities. Resentment sets in.

Understanding Each Other

As a couple, read through this list of ways people respond when they've been hurt or misunderstood or are facing a crisis. After each statement, discuss how each of you typically responds and how that reaction impacts your spouse. Determine ahead of time not to blame your partner for what you perceive to be a negative response. Try praying, "Lord, help us to understand each other better."

- I tend to hold grudges a long time.
- I let go of my anger and resentment toward my partner or toward the situation eventually, maybe even fairly soon, but not immediately. I keep it up long enough to make sure my spouse knows that he or she has wronged me and that I'm not happy about it.
- In my mind and heart, I relive the grievance repeatedly and allow bitterness and resentment to develop—especially if my partner has been a real jerk and doesn't even recognize how upset I am.
- I know I'm too easily offended.
- My response depends on how bad the action of my spouse was. I believe certain actions shouldn't be easily forgiven.
- I instantly forgive my partner because I have been forgiven.

The Perfect Example

Think back to the day Jesus was crucified. While on the cross, Jesus said, "'Father, forgive them, for they don't know what they are doing.' And the soldiers gambled for his clothes by throwing dice" (Luke 23:34 NLT).

Christ had been through unthinkable pain. For him to make a statement like this makes no sense at all. Men whom his Father had created were mocking him. How could Jesus push up on the nails in his feet, sending excruciating pain throughout his body, and suck in the breath to audibly forgive these people for such atrocities? His situation was totally unfair. It was humiliating, despicable, and sickening. But he forgave them.

Forgiveness Brings Healing

For Dan and Leigh, forgiving each other for the negative ways they responded to each other in the middle of unthinkable pain brought clearer vision. Leigh writes:

> Letters and cards came in telling us how Luke had touched and impacted lives. These letters helped Dan to focus on Luke's bright life, and eventually, he found himself at the golf course again, practicing the game he and his son had greatly enjoyed together.
>
> We got word that Luke's heart went to a police officer; his pancreas and one of his kidneys went to a woman who had suffered from juvenile diabetes. His other kidney went to a young mom; his eyes helped people with vision issues, and his skin went to burn victims. His liver went to a man serving as a missionary pastor in Alaska. We knew Luke's final wish was to help people—and he did that in life-giving ways through organ donation.
>
> Together, Dan and I were eventually able to embrace the good that came out of our great tragedy. Earlier, it had been hard to forgive God for allowing this accident to happen. The idea that God is good and that he is trustworthy seemed far removed from what took place. We both know there are

things we won't ever understand in this lifetime, but we can still choose forgiveness and love over bitterness and blame.

A Marker Moment

Dan and Leigh are quick to admit they had a long journey through misunderstandings in communication, but one of their first steps toward forgiving each other came at an unlikely time. They waited three weeks to pick up Luke's ashes. At the mortuary that day, they walked in holding hands, approached the desk, and signed the papers. Then they were given their son's urn. "As the mortuary attendant handed Dan the beautifully carved box," Leigh said, "I looked at it and said, 'How is *this* my son?'"

They walked out to the car, and Dan handed the box to Leigh so he could drive. Leigh says:

> I felt the weight in my arms, and my thoughts went to the day I carried my ten pound, two ounce baby boy home from the hospital. His weight was about the same as the box of ashes I now held.
>
> No parents should have to carry their child in a box; children are supposed to outlive their parents. At first the tears came slowly, then in torrents—deep, soundless sobs, with my head bent over my son's remains. Sorrow shook my whole body, like a silent tsunami.
>
> Dan gently reached over and touched my hand and held it tightly. His own voice overflowing with deep sorrow and emotion, he said, "I know, honey, I know."
>
> For the first time since Luke's death, I felt a connection—a deep human connection in our grief, something no other

person on earth would know. My husband was torn apart and broken. Perhaps not in the exact same way I was, but the common ground of our grief was the love of our only son.

Without using words like "I'm sorry," or "Please forgive me," we were beginning to forgive each other for our outrageous behaviors following Luke's death. We were showing our understanding that grief is a very complex, messy, and emotional thing.

Through GriefShare, I learned that we each bring our own issues of emotional brokenness into marriage. If these issues have not been healed and resolved by the grace of Jesus before a crisis strikes, they will most definitely spill out when we are emotionally raw, spent, and broken. God promises: "The LORD is close to the brokenhearted; he rescues those whose spirits are crushed" (Ps. 34:18 NLT). Dan and I were both severely brokenhearted and crushed in spirit, but we went on to claim the next verse: "The righteous person faces many troubles, but the LORD comes to the rescue each time" (v. 19 NLT).

That day was a milestone—a marker moment. Dan and I knew that through both our prayers and our repentance after fleshly fallouts and arguments, and with emotional baggage spilling out, we would forgive each other and move forward one baby step at a time. Our long journey was imperfect, and even sinful at times, but we knew his grace would meet us each step of the way.

Forgiveness in Marriage

When Carol and I (Gene) don't feel like forgiving each other for hurt feelings as we continue to walk through the ongoing journey of Jason's incarceration, one of the most helpful things we do is to turn to the Bible and find Scripture on the importance of genuine forgiveness. Those verses have led us to several principles, and although the wording of those principles below is ours, we think the concepts themselves are clearly biblical.

Keep short accounts.

> Be gentle with one another, sensitive. Forgive one another as quickly and thoroughly as God in Christ forgave you. (Eph. 4:32 MSG)

Many times in our marriage when I've found resentment building in me, I've had to ask: *How can I be gentle to my wife and be sensitive to her needs when she has offended me with her words?* Something that works for us: I know she loves coffee, and I've developed the daily habit of getting up early enough to make coffee and bring it to her in bed. There's something in that simple act of kindness that melts unforgiveness between us. We instantly realize that we're on the same team. We set the alarm an hour earlier than necessary to carve out this time for coffee and verbal connection. We talk about issues before they fester.

Apologize and talk about what happened.

> But if we confess our sins to him, he is faithful and just to forgive us our sins and to cleanse us from all wickedness. (1 John 1:9 NLT)

It's important for me to confess my sins to God. I also think it's important—I'm still learning this—to apologize to my wife quickly when I've been short-tempered over stress related to Jason's incarceration. That apology is an unmistakable sign to her that I'm genuinely sorry for my explosive or inappropriate behavior. It enables us to avoid the silent treatment—and I hate the silent treatment! If we don't talk about the issue, we might be "not talking" to each other for hours or even for a couple of days—until we forget why we aren't communicating.

Practice automatic forgiveness.

> "Master, how many times do I forgive a brother or sister who hurts me? Seven?"
>
> Jesus replied, "Seven! Hardly. Try seventy times seven." (Matt. 18:21–22 MSG)

Because Carol and I live in a challenging situation that will probably not end in our lifetime, we've had to learn that forgiveness usually isn't a onetime thing. We're still human. Tempers flare. We disagree about key decisions. We communicate poorly when we're exhausted. We tend to blame each other for the problem. In any of those circumstances, we're learning to instantly recognize that this negativity and unforgiveness could escalate. So we STOP and remind ourselves:

- We want resolution.
- We need the support of each other, or our marriage won't survive.
- Our love is deeper than this crisis.
- We're committed to forgiving each other for negative behaviors and outbursts quickly and often.

Often when we've had an "incident," I put my arms around Carol and whisper in her ear, "We're on the same team."

She usually responds, "Please forgive me for overreacting."

And yes! We have to do that over and over and over again.

Be unoffendable.

> Forgive as quickly and completely as the Master forgave you. And regardless of what you put on, wear love. It's your basic, all-purpose garment. Never be without it. (Col. 3:13–14 MSG)

Once Carol and I were in the rhythm of living in our difficult circumstances, we had to make a conscious decision to choose *love,* instead of *blame,* as a first response. Eventually, I started to realize that when she lashed out with an inappropriate response, her reaction was coming out of her deep pain, not out of anger toward me. That's when we began asking God to help us to be *unoffendable.* It's hard to master, but it's worth the effort.

Seek help.

> Love prospers when a fault is forgiven. (Prov. 17:9 NLT)

You may be reading through this list thinking: *Our marriage is too far gone. I don't know how we could ever get to a place of apologizing, keeping short accounts, or being unoffendable.* That's what Leigh thought while consumed with the sorrow connected to her son's death. She turned to GriefShare and found a support group that helped her begin to take important next steps that could move her in the direction of healing, forgiveness, and reconciliation with Dan. You may find a support group in your church, or you may want to seek pastoral counseling. In some cases, the wounds are so multifaceted and the negative patterns of blame, unforgiveness, bitterness, and anger so deep-rooted that professional counseling is necessary before restoration can take place. To find a Christian counselor, go to Christian Care Connect.[4] Taking action is essential!

Unexpected Comfort

Six months after Luke's death, a group of women in Leigh's church invited her to go to a Christian women's conference in Portland, Oregon. Family finances were tight, and she didn't feel comfortable leaving Dan alone. So she shared her concerns with him. He sweetly told her that she should go, that it was important to feed and nurture her soul. While she was there, he texted her daily, asking how she was and letting her know he missed her.

The day she was to come home, their daughter Marisa called Dan and invited them to come for dinner as soon as Leigh arrived. Dan called Leigh beforehand to prepare her: Marisa was going to try to get them to take a little dog home with them. An abandoned dog had broken through Marisa's fence and walked right into their home through an open door. Even before meeting the dog, Dan said, "Leigh, we just can't take a dog right now. We have too much," meaning that they had experienced too much emotional turmoil as a result of Luke's death. Leigh agreed with him.

She agreed, that is, until she got to her daughter's home that night. At the front door, she met an adorable little Yorkie with a crooked ear and a long, lopsided tail. He was imperfectly beautiful. The little dog's cuteness didn't budge Dan—he still didn't want the dog. But when he saw how Leigh bonded with this furry bundle of joy, he agreed that they could take him home.

In fact, it was Dan who named the dog: Skeeter—short for *mosquito*, because that little dog sucked the love right out of them (or perhaps injected it into them). Little Skeeter became a healing gift to both of them.

The Benefits of Forgiveness

Lewis B. Smedes says, "When we forgive we set a prisoner free and then discover that the prisoner we set free was us."[5] When we forgive our spouse for emotionally hurting us or for judging us because we respond to painful circumstances differently, we set the tone for a happier marriage.

Forgiveness doesn't negate the wrong done to you; it sets you free from bitterness and anger. Forgiveness allows you to move forward—out of the hurts of the past and toward a productive, joy-filled marriage.

Some of the benefits of forgiveness are learning to laugh again, better health, and renewed closeness.

Learning to Laugh Again

Dan and Leigh eventually recovered their sense of humor. She says, "We just love to be silly and goofy together." Because of an accident when she was thirteen, Leigh wears a brace on her left foot and ankle. She jokingly calls it her "lucky leg," and because she sometimes has trouble walking, Dan often thoughtfully asks if she needs help.

On a trip to Palm Springs with Leigh's sister and brother-in-law, Dan and Leigh were enjoying dinner in a restaurant that had great music. Her sister said, "I feel like dancing."

Dan looked at Leigh, winked, and said, "Well, what do you say, would you like me to spin you on your lucky leg?" They all laughed so hard tears rolled down their cheeks. Leigh said, "It felt so good to belly laugh and leave all the heavy emotions behind, at least for that moment. For us, laughter is such wonderful medicine." She's right. Job 8:21 says, "He will yet fill your mouth with laughter and your lips with shouts of joy."

Better Health

Mayo Clinic reports that letting go of grudges and bitterness can clear the way for improved health and peace of mind. Their researchers say forgiveness leads to "healthier relationships, improved mental health, less anxiety, stress and hostility, lower blood pressure, fewer symptoms of depression, a stronger immune system, improved heart health, and improved self-esteem."[6] All of those benefits help couples to have healthier marriages too.

Renewed Closeness

Robert Quillen said, "A happy marriage is the union of two good forgivers."[7] Unforgiveness between hurting marriage partners brings loneliness, misunderstanding, judgment, and increased pain. But forgiveness brings healing, comfort, companionship, shared insight for important decision-making, tender human touch, spiritual unity, and an ability to focus on a future beyond the crisis. Forgiveness restores both the hope that your marriage will make it and the anticipation that you will once again experience shared joy.

Moving Forward

Forgiveness is not forgetting the pain, nor is it approving the wrong actions of your spouse. Forgiveness does not erase the memory of what has happened, nor does it mean everything will turn out perfectly.

Mark Twain is credited with this quote: "Forgiveness is the fragrance the violet sheds on the heel that has crushed it." In the end, because we want our marriage to have staying power, Carol and I have made a choice. We're not giving up on each other. We're in this together—and we've made the decision to give and receive forgiveness from each other as often as needed. Sometimes that's every day. And that's okay.

Discussion Questions *for* Couples and Small Groups

1. What was your main take-away from this chapter?
2. Reread the list on page 86 of ways people respond when they've been hurt or misunderstood or are

facing a crisis. Which one do you most identify with? Why?

3. Ephesians 4:32 (MSG) says, "Be gentle with one another, sensitive. Forgive one another as quickly and thoroughly as God in Christ forgave you." How difficult is it for you and your spouse to keep short accounts? Discuss.
4. The chapter states, "Forgiveness is not forgetting the pain." If you keep remembering the pain someone else caused you, how is it possible to forgive? Discuss.
5. What benefits have you received as a result of forgiving your spouse quickly?

CHAPTER 5

The Right Word at the Right Time

> Words are like seeds. Once planted in your mate's life, your words will bring forth flowers or weeds, health or disease, healing or poison. You carry a great responsibility for their use.
>
> —Dennis and Barbara Rainey

It happened again. Carol and I (Gene) were in the car running errands, and she was waving her arms making sounds intended to point out that I was too close to the car in front of us. When that car slowed down, she shrieked, "Watch out!" I slammed on the brakes, and we were jolted forward against the seat belts.

As usual, I'd had plenty of room to stop. We could have avoided this jerky outcome if she hadn't overreacted. I was upset with her for being a backseat driver—again. Carol was defensive. "I screamed because I honestly thought we were in danger, and I believed my warning might save our lives."

I was unconvinced. I pulled the car to the side of the road, looked in her direction, and sarcastically said, "Do you want to drive?"

I admit it—poor attitude and poor choice of words. As a result, my wife shut down. Still idling there at the roadside, I watched tears trickle down Carol's cheeks. She quickly slipped into her silent martyr role. I eventually realized that if we were going to get home that day, I needed to drive. The rest of the day was clouded with the thick silence of anger, hurt, and misunderstanding.

Later, Carol explained, "I wasn't trying to tell you how to drive or to make you feel like an inadequate driver. My scream was involuntary."

The biggest challenge to our marriage has been the crisis of our son's arrest. But long before that, I was already learning that poorly chosen words can have a lasting impact on my wife—for an hour, a day, a series of days, or much longer. And when we're in the middle of a crisis, both of us—and probably you too—are more prone to take offense at poorly chosen words.

I (Carol) am a pastor's kid and grew up in a pastor's home. When Gene and I became engaged, my dad instructed us on how to have a happy marriage—including the importance of well-chosen words. He mentioned a couple he'd counseled after they survived a horrific automobile accident. The husband walked away with minor injuries, but his wife had to be removed from the passenger side by the Jaws of Life and taken by ambulance to the hospital where she had surgery and was placed in the intensive care unit. The accident left her with severe facial scarring.

Once, in the middle of a heated argument, Jose looked at his wife, Maria, and said, "You old, scar-faced woman—can't you do *anything* right?" It was as if a bomb dropped in the room. From that point on, even though Jose apologized profusely, Maria imagined whenever Jose looked at her that he saw only her scars—not her personality, her intelligence, or her spiritual depth. She said, "During intimate moments with my husband, when my heart longed to be fully accepted and loved, I was afraid he could only see my ugly scars. I shut down emotionally and pushed him away. I couldn't 'unhear' those cruel words he'd said."

That day my father reminded us of an important verse of Scripture in Ephesians 4:29: "Do not let any unwholesome talk come out of your mouths, but only what is helpful for building others up according to their needs, that it may benefit those who listen." He reminded us that words can hurt, and words can heal—and we needed to choose the right words at the right time to experience a happy marriage and to make it through the tough spots in life.

Becoming Teammates

Brenda Yoder, author of *Fledge: Launching Your Kids without Losing Your Mind*, has been willing to speak openly about her early married years. Her story reminds us that the mid-marriage crisis isn't always an accident, a health issue, a death, or a single shocking experience. It can be a seasonal change in your family—such as having a strong-willed teenager emerge, causing your long-established communication patterns to suddenly blow up, resulting in major stress in your marriage. Brenda says:

> My marriage is like the movie *My Big Fat Greek Wedding*. I am half Italian and the youngest of four girls. As I was growing up, there was no shortage of dramatic or animated words in my family. I assumed that most families exploded with words, and that everyone knew the others didn't mean half of it.
>
> As the youngest, I looked up to my teenage sisters, longing to be acknowledged by them, rather than routinely reminded that I was the baby. My desire to have a voice in the family food chain morphed into an eating disorder, both anorexia and bulimia, from the time I was a young teen until marriage. My body demonstrated the message I wanted others to hear: "See me."
>
> Marriage at twenty-one was a haven from the eating disorder that consumed so much of my time and energy. My high-school and college sweetheart, a quiet farm boy from a conservative family of all boys, saw beyond my problem. He did see me, and I was excited to start our new life together. As I learned to cope better with food and weight, I didn't yet realize that food both stuffed and starved my emotions. As a young bride overcoming an eating disorder, I reverted to the unhealthy communication patterns I'd learned growing up. I was dramatic and explosive.
>
> At times of conflict, my words exploded, and I assumed my husband would figure out which ones I meant. A man of few words, he would often shut down or get defensive in the face of that onslaught of words and emotion, and in response I would ramp up even more, fighting for my need to be heard and understood.

We added one, two, three, and four kids to our family, and during that time our patterns of communication showed no improvement. Though we had a healthy marriage when there was no conflict, it was unhealthy and explosive when communication broke down.

Then our son became a teenager. My reactionary and explosive words eventually created a disaster in our family as I became a reactive parent who got into power struggles with our teen. I would argue with my husband for not taking my side or stepping in when I thought he should. He would retreat even more. Our marriage became fragile, and for several years it felt as if our family was falling apart, past the point of no return.

I knew that I couldn't blame my husband or our son for my behavior, even though we each contributed to the problem. As heads of a two-career family with four kids active in sports, my husband and I never found time for counseling. Under the stress of too much responsibility and too little time, we would fight, then say we were sorry, and vow to do better the next day. Often, I'd lie in bed crying, and my husband would simply say, "We'll get through this."

I made a career change that provided a positive turning point for my emotional health and that of our family. But twenty years of poor communication in marriage had left scars. As our family healed, it became more evident that our dysfunctional communication in marital conflict was not just an emotional battle but a spiritual one. I still reacted with anger and harsh words when I felt unheard, and my husband would withdraw or get defensive in response.

One of our arguments took place in our laundry room. At an impasse, I suddenly realized that we both wanted the same outcome. Five words kept coming to mind. I finally said them out loud: "We're on the same team."

Those words clicked for both of us. We realized we were fighting over something we both desired—our child's best interest. Since then, the sense of being on the same team has helped both of us forge healthier communication patterns as we approach the empty-nest years. We are on the same team, wanting the best for our kids, each other, and our future.

Since we've redefined our marriage strategy and see ourselves as teammates, I am better able to know what to do with my words when my emotions are triggered or I don't feel heard. I've learned to communicate my needs without blaming my husband. He's learning to share his needs without fear of being attacked. For so many years, it felt like we were against each other, competing for divergent goals. I take ownership for the hurtful words I spewed in those early years of our marriage. But I've learned that healing words are more powerful—words such as "I'm sorry," "I love you," and "We're on the same team."

We've both come toward the middle with our communication. He says more and I say less, and both of us are more likely to use words that are helpful rather than harmful. Often, the best words either of us say in a conversation that's about to go wrong is, "We're on the same team."

An Assessment

I (Gene) think I communicated poorly in the early years of our marriage because of my father's negative example. I don't remember having a heart-to-heart talk with him about anything. Other people talked about father/son bonding, but I had no idea what that was.

I never heard my dad say he was proud of me, that I'd made a good decision, or that I was handling life well. He was a harsh disciplinarian, and he abused my mother, yelled constantly at my two brothers and me, drank too much, and wasn't home very often. I graduated from high school as the runner-up to the salutatorian, but he never complimented me on my excellent grades. He showed little respect for women, and I never heard him speak words of affirmation to my mother. He basically lived each day for whatever brought him pleasure.

Instead of following in my father's footsteps, I determined at an early age that I would be a different kind of a husband—that I would encourage Carol, respect her, love her, listen to her, and value her opinions. In spite of that decision, at times I found myself slipping into my father's negative speech patterns.

Carol and I made up our minds to be aware of the words we were speaking to each other and the tone of voice we used so we wouldn't fall into hurtful communication patterns. There are certain questions we would ask ourselves to help "keep us honest." We've created the following assessment containing questions much like those we use that we hope will help you evaluate how you communicate with your spouse.

True or False?

As a couple, read these statements and honestly discuss whether they are true or false about your use of words.

- Sometimes I hear my father's or mother's voice coming out of my mouth.
- When I'm upset, I withdraw into silence and noncommunication.

- I tend to be reactive and explosive when my spouse gets on my nerves.
- It's hard for me to say, "I'm sorry."
- I often talk first and think later.
- I try to say something good about my partner when we have a disagreement.
- It's hard for me to change the verbal way I've always responded to stress.
- When I try to explain what I'm thinking to my spouse, I often feel like he/she isn't listening.
- I am quick to use words of affirmation, love, and encouragement.

Is Change Possible?

After divorcing my mother, my father married two more times. Both of those marriages brought him several stepchildren. Dad passed away a few years ago, and my brothers and I attended his funeral, along with his third wife and her children. At the memorial service, the microphone was open for anyone who wanted to share a few memories about Dad.

One by one, his younger stepchildren stood up and spoke tearfully about how he encouraged them, was there for them, and was a godly example for them. My brothers and I looked at each other, amazed. Were they talking about the same father we had? What had happened to turn the abusive father we remembered into a kind and affirming man with a wife and children who mourned his passing?

I believe it was his godly wife and, no doubt, the passing of time that gave him a new perspective on life. She helped to rekindle a faith that had lain dormant in his heart for many years. Love and care for others had come alive in him. *It's never too late to change,* I found myself thinking as I listened. My dad had become a new person in Christ; he'd learned to choose his words more carefully—and it made a major difference to his wife and to the people closest to him.

The Importance of Words

The Bible is filled with references to the importance of words. As you read through these verses as a couple, share which Scriptures are the most meaningful to you and why they're important at this time in your marriage.

- "May the words of my mouth and the meditation of my heart be pleasing to you, O Lord, my rock and my redeemer" (Ps. 19:14 NLT).
- "Some people make cutting remarks, but the words of the wise bring healing" (Prov. 12:18 NLT).
- "A gentle response defuses anger, but a sharp tongue kindles a temper-fire" (Prov. 15:1 MSG).
- "Kind words heal and help; cutting words wound and maim" (Prov. 15:4 MSG).
- "Kind words are like honey—sweet to the soul and healthy for the body" (Prov. 16:24 NLT).
- "Watch your tongue and keep your mouth shut, and you will stay out of trouble" (Prov. 21:23 NLT).
- "A word fitly spoken is like apples of gold in settings of silver" (Prov. 25:11 NKJV).

- "Those who consider themselves religious and yet do not keep a tight rein on their tongues deceive themselves, and their religion is worthless" (James 1:26).
- "Don't grumble against one another, brothers and sisters, or you will be judged" (James 5:9).

Three Statements

Bill and Pam Farrel are good friends to Carol and me. They've visited our son in maximum-security prison, and they've encouraged us in our marriage relationship as we continue to navigate a journey that includes the incarceration of a loved one. They are also the bestselling authors of *Men Are Like Waffles and Women Are Like Spaghetti: Understanding and Delighting in Your Differences*. Pam and Bill have excellent advice on the importance of words.

Pam says:

> I am an enthusiastic entrepreneur at heart. I take great joy in creating something from nothing and providing quality resources for others while simultaneously providing for my family.
>
> When Bill, only twenty-eight years old, was new in his senior pastor position, I was a mom at home completing my education. Tuition was stressing our already tight budget, so I attended a seminar on starting a business. The presenter was very persuasive. I bought the magic beans.
>
> But on the way home, I began to feel convicted by the Holy Spirit. I had spent more than I should have. In fact, Bill and I had agreed that for any expenditure over a certain amount,

we would decide as a team if this was how *we* wanted to spend *our* money. I had violated that trust. I prayed for forgiveness and wisdom on the best way to tell my husband.

I walked in, took Bill's hand, and looked him in the eyes. With emotion, I said, "I have something to tell you, and you aren't going to like it, but please tell me 'I love you and we will get through this together.'" Then I went on to confess my transgression. As I spoke, I could see Bill's anger rising, but to his credit, he said through gritted teeth, "Pam, I love you, I forgive you, and we will get through this together."

The mercy Bill gave me that day lodged deep in my heart, and my love for him grew even stronger.

Years later, my father passed away and left me an inheritance. Bill was offered "an incredible investment opportunity" by someone, and Bill talked me into investing my money toward our future needs.

Today, people are more skeptical of investment advisers—there have been so many financial fraud cases in recent history. But our investment decision was made before all that.

One day, our adviser took our money and ran. Bill was horrified to learn that it was all gone. But his biggest regret was talking me into investing it in the first place. My treasured inheritance from my father! He prayed about how to break the news.

Bill came home, took my hand, and with sorrow in his eyes, said, "Pam, I have something to tell you, and you aren't going to like it, but I need you to tell me 'I love you and we will get through this together.'" As I listened to his news, I remembered Bill's grace and mercy for me those many years before. In spite of our loss, my heart pushed out the words, "Bill, I love you, I forgive you, and we will get through this together."

After facing, early in their marriage, what could have been a huge falling out over finances, they had made a pre-decision: They would be quick to offer the right words at the right time in the future. They chose honesty, along with words of love and forgiveness, over strife and anger. Because of that, they became stronger as a married couple. They had learned to say, "I love you. I forgive you. We will get through this together."

Pam says:

> Words of grace, mercy, and forgiveness create an environment where love can accumulate interest just like money in an investment account. In such a positive environment, a relationship can flourish emotionally and spiritually (and perhaps even financially) because you will be functioning as a team, learning to accept each other's mistakes and moving on from them together.[1]

The Wrong Words at the Wrong Time

When Carol and I were first married, she initiated a discussion about loyalty and what it meant to her. One of her most vivid memories from her growing-up years involved her family having dinner in the home of friends from church. Most of the children were running around having fun, as kids do, but Carol was in the kitchen helping with the final meal preparations. The adults were all talking in the kitchen.

It was a hot summer day, and Mrs. Johnson was wearing a short-sleeved dress. She struggled with weight issues. Carol said, "I watched her husband walk over to his wife, who was dripping with perspiration at the stove. Mrs. Johnson lifted her arm as she reached for a spatula. Mr. Johnson grasped the loose flesh under her arm and jiggled it back and forth as he said, "I think it's time for us to work on the battle of the bulge." Mrs. Johnson's face turned red. She was obviously deeply hurt by his cruel comment. My parents looked embarrassed, said they needed to check on their kids, and left the kitchen.

Carol said, "From that point on, I knew that one of the most important issues for me when I married would be my husband's loyalty—I wanted a spouse who would not put me down with unkind words, either in public or in private."

Carol's cousin Kathy was happy. It was September of 1978 and life was going well, even though, like most college-age couples, she and her husband Bob were broke. They had just moved out of married housing at Ferris State University in Big Rapids, Michigan. They had a sweet, one-year-old daughter, Jennifer, and they were expecting their next child in January.

Kathy says:

> I had some abnormal bleeding on Jennifer's first birthday. I called the doctor and heeded his advice to take it easy. A few days later, the contractions started—at twenty-two weeks, far too early, my mom took me to the hospital where Bob met us. The doctors were able to stop the contractions with medication and positioned my bed with my head down and my body angling uphill. I was willing to do anything to keep my baby from being born too early.

I remember thinking and praying, "Thy will be done" and really meaning it. Several hours later I woke up with hard, close contractions, and I was whisked to the labor and delivery area in the hospital. Bob was called and made it in time for the birth of our son, Robert (Robbie) Peter Jr. He was perfect, just way too small. He tried to breathe once, and his heart continued beating for four hours before he died. Through our tears, we held him, looked at his beautiful face, and marveled at how much he looked like his daddy. Our sorrow was overwhelming.

We were surrounded by our parents and church family, who held us up in prayer and comforted us with their words. At ages twenty-three and twenty-four, we had to make funeral arrangements for our child and find a cemetery plot. Bob went alone to the funeral home to pick out a casket because I was still in the hospital. When Bob returned, he said, "I know we're struggling financially, but I got the middle-priced one because the least expensive casket was made of Styrofoam and looked like a cooler." When I saw it later, I was struck that it was the size of my sewing machine box.

Bob's mom was with us in the hospital that day, and when Bob told us about the casket, she said, "It was foolish to spend that much money. You should have gone with the cheapest casket." Her words were so hurtful. We couldn't bury our baby boy in a cooler.

Then the clerk came with the blank birth certificate to be filled out. I told her our son was named after his daddy, Robert Peter Jr. She asked, "Are you sure you want to give *this* baby *that* name?" It felt like she was saying, "Are you sure you want to waste your husband's name on a dead baby?" Of the many hurtful comments made to us over the next few weeks, that was one of the worst.

But there were others. Bob and I became a team to protect our hearts from hurtful words. It was as if the thoughtless words of others propelled us into speaking words of comfort to each other—and that brought us closer together. The words spoken by our pastor at Robbie's funeral on a sunny fall day comforted us the most:

> I will lift up my eyes to the hills—
> From whence comes my help?
> My help comes from the LORD,
> Who made heaven and earth. (Ps. 121:1–2 NKJV)

Kathy and Bob are committed to nurturing their marriage with life-giving words. Today Kathy is a certified bereavement support nurse, in addition to working as an OB/GYN office nurse. She reaches out with healing words to all of her patients who have had losses.

Picking the Right Words

Here are some general principles that work for us:

Practice loyalty in your public speech toward or about your spouse.

The mocking and critical words Mr. Johnson directed toward his wife in the scene a few pages ago were disloyal. Make sure that when others hear you speak to or about your spouse, they hear only respect, admiration, and affection, whether your spouse is present or not. If you feel critical toward your spouse, then that's a good reminder that whatever negative words you were about to say would be best said not in public but rather in a private setting, spoken carefully so that they are edifying rather than hurtful, and balanced with praise. And even then, ask yourself: *Am I speaking out of love and in my spouse's best interest, or am I indulging my own selfish interest?*

Use words that are affirming, caring, and encouraging.

Carol says, "When Gene tells me I did a good job speaking at an event, I feel supported by my best friend. When I tell him what an incredible father he is to Jason—he knows I appreciate all that he does to be an encouragement to our incarcerated son, and it's good for him to know that someone notices the time and effort it takes to be supportive." When Carol was involved with directing women's ministries in our church, I (Gene) would say, "You're a gifted leader and I'm proud of you."

Mother Teresa said, "Kind words can be short and easy to speak, but their echoes are truly endless."

Carol's mother recently passed away, and I know what a great loss this is to my wife. The two of us were on a walk yesterday and I said, "I know you miss calling your mother and asking for her advice. We know she's in heaven, but I know your heart still hurts." She grabbed my hand with unspoken appreciation, and I knew my words were healing to her heart.

When I use words that reassure, cheer, buoy up, support, and raise the spirits of my wife, she knows she's married to her best cheerleader. We affirm our loyalty and commitment to each other. When we make the long drive to the prison to visit our son, we speak to each other our commitment that we're in this long-term life situation together and we couldn't make it without the encouragement we give to each other.

Think before you speak.

How often have you heard, when someone says something that hurts another's feelings, "I just didn't think . . ." How true. We too often don't think before we open our mouths how those words may affect those to whom we're speaking or who are within earshot—and when it's your spouse whose feelings are at stake, the potential for disaster is multiplied. A spoken word can't be retrieved—and whether it's accusatory and harsh or loving and supportive, it will long be remembered. It's best to avoid sentences that begin with accusations: "You always . . ." or "You never . . ." Practice honesty spoken with tenderness when dealing with sensitive issues.

Shelter your spouse from blame; include your spouse in praise.

If those around you should, for any reason, begin to address your spouse negatively, whether in accusation or criticism or disrespect, become your spouse's defender and verbal bodyguard: "Hey, John—I don't think that's true at all. You're being unfair. If you've got an issue you think you need to bring up, then do it in a respectful tone and skip the inflammatory language. And if you can't do that, then this isn't the time or place."

If you're in public and someone is lavishing praise on you, share it with your spouse if you can. Not long ago someone was congratulating Cindy that the book *Unplanned* that she wrote collaboratively with Abby Johnson had been made into a movie that was about to be released.[2] "Thank you," she said, "and actually, Dave had a hand in that book too—he was the editor and wrote some of the scenes."

Practice words of gratitude and respect.

When I thank Carol for making a delicious meal or when she compliments me on grilling a perfect salmon filet, we feel uplifted by each other. Make a daily habit of thanking each other for small acts of kindness.

Make your words to your spouse a verbal caress.

Make your tone of voice gentle, warm, loving. Select words that will seem to your spouse as welcome and reassuring as a caress. Make it your goal to leave your spouse smiling, sorry the moment had to end, and looking forward to your next time together. It doesn't take any extra effort to make this happen—just be intentional about it and be completely present in that moment, not distracted or preoccupied but fully engaged in communicating positively to the one you love and who loves you.

And when you're offering that warm verbal caress—add to its power with eye contact and a lingering physical touch as well. Triple whammy!

A Final Word

In his bestselling book *The Blessing*, Gary Smalley reminds us that "a spoken message of love and acceptance" is one of the most powerful ways we can bless our loved ones.[3] I want to be the person who does that for my wife. For all of us who travel difficult roads in the middle of less-than-ideal circumstances, there's one sure thing: if we use words of love, thanksgiving, appreciation, affirmation, and respect when we communicate with our spouse, we'll find joy in the middle of the toughest journey—because we'll know we're on the same team!

Discussion Questions
for Couples and Small Groups

1. What action step will you take as a result of reading this chapter?
2. Pages 105–6 contain a list of true/false questions about communication. Which do you identify with most, and why?
3. There's a list of general principles we recommend for communication with and about your spouse on pages 113–16. Which one of those describes an area in which you need significant improvement? Explain.
4. Proverbs 12:18 (NLT) says, "Some people make cutting remarks, but the words of the wise bring healing." Share a time when the words of your spouse brought healing.

CHAPTER 6

An Articulate Silence

> Who would think that muteness could be so eloquent? That blindness could open so many eyes? . . .
>
> If you will not look away, you will see something of what was revealed in the straw and swaddling clothes of the manger.
>
> You will see the power of the powerless.
>
> —Ken Gire

I (Dave) am a writer, and writers like words. We experiment with placing them together in a variety of ways, selecting first one word and then replacing it with a different one, placing them in a different order, in short sentences and long. For us, words and then more words are usually the answer to everything. Or else what are books for? Books make no sound, and most of them have no pictures. They don't move. Their value is simply in the words on the page and the meanings behind those words, nothing else.

Just think of the phrases from our everyday speech that underline the importance of words in relationships:

We have to talk.

Talk to me.

Text me.

Call me.

I'd like to give him a piece of my mind.

You're going to have to explain that to me.

And yet. Words aren't the answer to every crisis—they can't be, because sometimes words are a tool that just isn't available to us.

Sometimes, our toolbox contains no words, only silence.

And for a writer, that's a little bit like those dreams where you're in public and suddenly realize that you're naked.

A few days ago, Cindy and I were driving through an older area near downtown Grand Rapids, Michigan—an area where none of the houses are less than several decades old and most of them are huge old Victorian places, perched near the street behind tiny yards, down at the heels, and now subdivided into apartments or group homes. Despite the cold and the icy sidewalks, there was a fair amount of foot traffic out that day, and most of those trudging along looked as if they might be headed home from work for lunch, some of them most likely headed back to group homes where adults who need supervision live semiautonomously.

As we waited for a light to change, I watched two men who appeared to be in their forties but also could have been much younger. They had the appearance of men who had lived difficult lives with too little money, too little food, and perhaps sometimes not a safe bed to sleep in or a roof over their heads. They were dressed in several mismatched layers of clothes that, if not rags, at least had seen better days. They crossed with the light, and the taller man, thin as a post, stood stoically waiting to cross the second street, thin face staring straight ahead, gloveless hands jammed into his pockets. The man beside him, at least a foot shorter, had the body shape and facial deformities we associate with those mentally disabled since birth with some congenital condition. His expression cherubic, a ragged knit cap pulled down tight over his head, he stood not just next to his taller friend but as if he wanted to melt into him, one hand tucked under his friend's arm, his head leaning against the man's shoulder except when he looked up at his friend's face to speak, which was often, since he seemed to be talking almost constantly.

With the windows rolled up against the cold, I couldn't hear what the smaller man was saying, but I could read his expression: it was clear that his affection for, his devotion to, his friend was total, something like that of a young child toward a beloved parent or sibling. And maybe they were siblings, since they appeared to be about the same age. They clearly weren't strangers or mere acquaintances—the taller man made no attempt to shake the other man off his arm or to distance himself.

The storyteller in me could spin out at least a half-dozen story lines to explain and flesh out the relationship between the two men. But even without knowing such details, a few things were clear. One was that the smaller man used his words, or at least his vocalizations, as well as his touch, to express his closeness to the taller man. The taller man never spoke in those few moments I observed them, but it was clear in the way he shepherded the other across the street and allowed his physical closeness that he was the one to accept responsibility for the other. Even without speaking, he was the protector. The leader. The provider and nurturer.

The light changed. We drove on, and the two men crossed the street, the shorter still clinging to the taller.

Cindy was driving that day, even though I'm the usual default driver. Why? Because we were just driving away from the hospital where I'd had a minor outpatient surgery. It had been done under general anesthetic, so I wouldn't be good to drive until the next day. I'm sure we spoke as we drove along—after all, we had an hour and a half drive home. But imagine for a minute that Cindy said not a word that whole day—not as she kissed me goodbye as they wheeled me down the hall toward the operating room, not as she sat with me in recovery, not as we drove home, and not as she prepared dinner and waited on me as I sat in a recliner with an ice pack. Imagine, further, that she *couldn't* speak—that she was mute. Would her day have been any less an expression of love if characterized only by her acts of sacrifice and tender care and not by the words we usually expect in such a situation?

St. Francis has often been "quoted" (incorrectly, no doubt, since this particular quotation didn't begin showing up until the 1990s) as saying: "Preach the gospel at all times. When necessary, use words." As illegitimate as that quotation no doubt is, there's truth in it. Cindy's tender care of me that day spoke her love more eloquently than any words would have. And even if she had not spoken at all, it would have been an articulate silence, freighted with love.

And that's what this chapter with the odd title is about—the many ways in which simple, caring actions and attitudes and nonverbal communications are as effective as and in some ways more effective than our words in caring for our loved ones, especially during times of crisis. Just as faith without deeds is dead (James 2:26), so a love not embodied by actions is lifeless as well.

"I Don't Trust Your Words!"

Ed was an MD, a surgeon. It had taken him close to ten years to get through college, med school, and residency. His wife, Greta, on the other hand, who had emigrated from Germany with her parents when she was twelve, had never gotten over the sense of inferiority regarding language she had formed during those first few years in the States when she was just learning English. She started college, met Ed there, and they married very young, in the summer after their sophomore year. But she dropped out in her junior year, ostensibly because a job opened up at their church that she wanted to take, and she thought they couldn't afford to *both* be in college and working only part time. Mostly, though, she dropped out because, despite her high IQ, she was terrified by the language requirements that went along with writing term papers, essay tests, class discussions, and so on. English was, after all, her second language. Her classmates used it so much better than she did. Or so she felt.

So maybe Ed shouldn't have been surprised when he discovered, a few years after he finished med school and joined the staff of a hospital on the West Coast, in an area where both of them had always wanted to live, that their marital disagreements often were completely dysfunctional, and even more so when their lives were threatened by such things as the serious illness of one of their young children and the bitter breakup of the church they loved. *We ought to be able to disagree as adults and work our way through it,* he thought. *We love each other. We're both believers. Why can't we just talk it through if we both stay calm?* So he would make every attempt to stay calm, think logically, present his thoughts—and could not figure out why halfway through his completely reasonable presentation, she would jump to her feet, cut him off with a slash of her hand, and say, "Stop! All these words—I don't trust them! You're just trying to manipulate and control me, just trying to get your way. I didn't finish college, you know—I speak German, not English [even though by that time she had spoken English as her daily language for more years than she had German], and I don't know all of those big words you geniuses with your doctorates know. I don't want to hear it!" And she wouldn't hear it, in fact, because then she would storm away, leaving Ed with half of his intended speech undelivered.

Was she right? Was Ed's method of delivering his side of the argument manipulative and controlling? Maybe. Surgeons are, after all, notoriously controlling and compulsive, even if they have the best intentions. (And when you're in surgery, don't you want a compulsive perfectionist holding the scalpel?) Frankly, in this chapter, it doesn't matter whether Ed or Greta was right. What's important is that for reasons of her own that made sense to her, Greta was unable to hear Ed's words. However logical, however wise, however loving—or not—they were, she just couldn't and wouldn't hear them.

You may suggest, *So stop arguing, Ed, and go love your wife—after you apologize, and then give her a hug.* Good suggestion—except that after things had gotten to that stage with Greta, days would pass in which she was in no mood to listen to anything Ed said, *and she refused to be touched.*

How, then, was Ed to bring their marriage back onto solid footing—without words and, in their case, without touch either? As someone who relied on words and logic to solve every issue that couldn't be resolved with a scalpel, how was Ed to bring healing to his marriage as he brought healing to his patients?

Fortunately, there are tools to use when words fail.

Your marriage may not feel like Ed and Greta's. You may be the kind of couple who talks everything out, until late into the night, to an extent that would exhaust mere mortals. But (and this is hard for a writer to say), words *can't* be your only tool in addressing the issues of marriage and life. Those issues are many and complex, and they hit you without warning like a broken tooth; you'll need a toolbox full of tools to respond effectively. If the only tool you use is verbal speech, there are many, like Greta, who will grow suspicious of your words. Many of the tools you can add to your toolbox have the power to be articulate even in their silence. In this chapter, we'll explore some of those, and I hope you'll use them often.

And remember: These tools are not simply for when you *can't* speak. In today's complex world, maintaining a strong relationship with your spouse requires more than words. It requires touch. It requires the ability to listen, even to what is not being said. It requires wisdom. It requires kindness.

In fact, as you read through the list that makes up the rest of this chapter, notice how so much of what we suggest here comes down to nothing more than kindness. "Be kind and compassionate to one another, forgiving each other, just as in Christ God forgave you," Paul exhorted us in Ephesians 4:32. How much of love comes down to something so simple—and so welcome—as kindness?

We've all heard of practicing "*random* acts of kindness." But in the context of nurturing a healthy marriage and serving your spouse, especially in times of crisis, there's nothing *random* about these acts. Even though they may sometimes be spontaneous, they're still deliberate and purposeful.

I've divided them into three categories: *thoughtful gestures, habits of love,* and *habits of life.*

Thoughtful Gestures

Make dinner. *But I'm not the cook!* you may object. *We divide the tasks in our house, and cooking is my wife's task. I mow the lawn.* Sorry, but I don't care. If your wife were laid up with a serious illness or injury, she wouldn't be doing the cooking, even if it *is* a task she normally performs. Sometimes you just have to pamper your spouse for no reason. So treat her as if she were laid up, unable to cook. Make dinner yourself. She'll be surprised and pleased even if it's burned or over-salted. It will be abundantly obvious to her, without even thinking about it, that it's the thought that counts. Even if the kids complain.

But seriously—I said *make* dinner. I didn't say *cook* it. If you're a rotten cook, you can always bring dinner home from her favorite restaurant or heat up something frozen. Or bring home the makings of subs and everyone can construct their own.

Your spouse may love cooking—but she can always cook tomorrow night. Tonight, she'll be happy to let herself be pampered.

Do the stuff your spouse hates to do—the stuff, in fact, that neither of you wants to do. Every marriage has those things. Maybe it's the finances. Or cooking. Or the laundry. Or yardwork. You may hate it yourself, but when you're trying to communicate love for your spouse without words, few things work better than just jumping in and doing the stuff your spouse hates without being asked—*especially* if it's stuff you hate yourself. Your spouse *knows* you hate it, which just means they'll appreciate it all the more.

And then don't make a big deal about it. The point is not for you to get pats on the back for being such a great person. It's to do something kind and loving for your spouse. The only reason to even tell your spouse about it would be so that they know they don't have to worry about it or do it—because you already did.

Leave your spouse a note. When my kids were small, my wife would put little love notes in their sack lunches. They'd open their lunch sack at school and there, next to the PB&J and the little bag of carrot sticks, would be a note saying, "Sarah—I know you'll do great today! Love you! Mom." Hard to imagine them reading those notes without a smile and a warm feeling.

You can do the same. A sticky note stuck on the mirror where you know she'll do her makeup: "You're already beautiful, just the way you are. I love you." Or in her suitcase she'll open in her hotel room on a business trip: "You'll knock 'em dead! I saw your PowerPoint presentation and it's great! Can't wait to welcome you home. All my love." Or stuck on the handle of the snow blower: "Do you realize how much I appreciate you getting all bundled up to go out into the cold to do this for us? I do! I love you for it—and for so much else."

Okay, technically, leaving a note is using words. So excuse me for breaking the rules—but it's still a good idea because it makes your spouse feel great.

And here's an idea from Carol Ensminger that uses no words whatsoever but that can't fail to touch your spouse: "At some point in our marriage, my husband, Michael, found a stone in the shape of a heart. After he found it, I would discover the heart in the most unexpected places. It has shown up in my lunchbox, under the neatly folded laundry, and in my suitcase when I travel. The little heart also shows up when there is strife in the marriage to remind me that I am loved and that his heart is mine."

Leave gas in the car. Coming home late from a long, tiring trip, the last thing you want to do is stop for gas just before you get home—especially if it's cold outside. You're already anticipating the warmth of home, of your favorite sloppy comfort clothes, of plopping down in front of the TV and turning on the game. *I can gas it up tomorrow,* you think. But the first one to use the car tomorrow may be your spouse. And then she'll have to fill it up herself.

Or—imagine her cranking up the car, checking the fuel gauge—and seeing that the tank is full. She knows you did that with her in mind. No words exchanged, and none needed. She knows, and she smiles.

That smile is what you're looking for in most of the things on this list. When life gets tough—when illness or financial difficulty strikes, when there are problems with the kids or your aging parents—you and your spouse might feel that you don't have much reason to smile. Give her a reason. It takes her out of the struggle, if only for a moment.

Habits of Love

Know your spouse's love language. If you haven't yet read Gary Chapman's bestselling *The 5 Love Languages: The Secret to Love That Lasts,*[1] now's the time. Understand which of those five languages (words of affirmation, quality time, receiving gifts, acts of service, and physical touch) are your spouse's top love languages. Always—especially during times of stress in your lives and marriage—find ways to express your love to your spouse *using his or her top love languages.*

And although it didn't make Gary Chapman's list, don't forget the one that the Lamberts include as the "extra credit" love language: eye contact. More on this later.

It's good to be aware, too, of what your own top love languages are. When the going gets rough, there's nothing wrong with reminding your spouse of what kinds of emotional support work best for you.

Go to bed together. Wake up together. No, I'm not talking about anything sexual, though it's probably not a bad idea. I'm just referring to the tendency in many of our modern and overtaxed marriages to keep somewhat different schedules. One of you has to get up earlier in the morning. One of you likes to stay up late enough to see the end of the basketball or football game or has a hard time turning off social media. And before you know it, "normal" is for one of you to be asleep in bed before the other even makes it as far as brushing their teeth, and one sleeps in an hour later than the other.

Change it up. Go out of your way to climb into bed some nights at the same time, and then to spend time cuddling, giving eye contact, touching, and following wherever all of that may lead. Then, some days, wake up together, too, and spend those few minutes with your arms around each other, mumbling sleepily. Not only does the touching count for a lot, the fact that you were willing to change your schedule to make it happen counts for a lot too.

Compromise. Somebody should write a book on marriage called *The Art of Compromise*. Just as nothing gets done in politics or business without it (that's what's being negotiated, after all, in negotiation), nothing gets done in marriage without willingness to compromise. A good working definition of *compromise* is that neither of you gets everything you want, but you both get something important to you.

Ed and Greta stumbled in this area too, just as they had with communication. Because Greta didn't trust Ed's words, meaningful negotiation when they disagreed became impossible. Finally, in an escalating argument one day over how to handle an issue with one of the kids, Greta jumped up and said, "Don't talk to me about compromise! Compromise just means I'm not getting what I want!"

Well—yeah. That's what compromise means, all right—that *neither* of you is getting all you want, so you negotiate to see what you're willing to give up.

In compromise, be willing to go further than you're comfortable with to enable your spouse to feel satisfied. That's what *love* means.

Make eye contact. This is so important I'm going to mention it a second time.

At the Lambert household, this often comes up at bedtime. Cindy will usually be in bed first, and when I come to bed and reach to turn out the bedside lamp, Cindy often says, "Wait! I'm sure you're desperate for a little eye contact." Meaning, of course, that she feels the need for some. And then she props her head on the pillow, her bright, eager face looking up, smiling expectantly and sweetly.

It may be late. I may be bushed. But what husband can refuse a look like that? And even if you can, you shouldn't. So we lie side by side for several minutes with the bedside lamp on, our heads on the pillow, maybe talking, maybe just looking into each other's eyes. Even if I wasn't aware of needing eye contact, I still find myself refreshed and affirmed.

And here's a distinction: This feels different for introverts than it does for extroverts. Extroverts usually want to look into the eyes of the person they're talking to. (I once talked to a man who changed churches just because, when they spoke face-to-face, the pastor of the first church tended to not look into his eyes.) Introverts, on the other hand, often experience intense eye contact as something of an intrusion, just as they would someone standing way too close to them or someone they just met giving them a bear hug.

Extroverts, extend some grace here—your introverted spouse may have limits on how much intense eye contact she can take. Introverts, be willing to experience some minor uneasiness in order to make sure your extroverted spouse gets the eye contact he craves.

Listen. Listen to your partner. When your spouse is speaking, give them your undivided and dedicated attention. Concentrate on hanging on every word, on reading between the lines, on paying attention to body language, on getting the big picture, including the emotional context. Use active listening techniques, repeating what your spouse said to make sure you got it right. (Men, I hate to say it, but you probably didn't get it right, so check to see where you went wrong.)

I read an account not long ago of an investigation into why one particular demographic group attends church less often in recent years. The answer—they didn't feel that they were being heard, being given a chance to tell their story, being listened to. Without that vital transaction, they lost interest and drifted away.

Not exactly what you want happening with your spouse.

As Paul Tillich says, "The first duty of love is to listen."

Give your partner some space. Sounds like a cliché, doesn't it? But imagine your spouse saying, "I need to go see the doctor today—my back's been really hurting me," and you saying in response, "Oh—can't it wait? I want us to get in some good together time today." No, of course you wouldn't do that. If your loved one needs care, you want them to get it, even if it means you'll be apart for a while. But we do something very similar when we deny them the time they need for a physical or mental health break apart from us. In truth, we all need occasional solitude, occasional freedom to choose where we'll go and what we'll do, when to rest and when to jump into action. It isn't that you don't love your spouse and want to spend time with her—it's just that occasionally you need to slink into your cave. Wives, sometimes you need a breather, too, either on your own or with your close friends, maybe over coffee, without hubby around for a change. And that's a good thing, not a bad thing.

When you send your spouse off to spend some time away from you, whether it's for a meal or the afternoon or the weekend or a week, there's a reward in it for you—you're likely to get your spouse back refreshed and relaxed and happy and eager to see you.

Hug back. Kiss back. Smile. Sometimes your spouse is the first one to think of expressing affection, of offering the hug or the kiss. That's your opportunity. Return that hug or kiss with warmth and enthusiasm. *Smile* while you're doing it.

One of the saddest scenes in film is in the 1993 Merchant Ivory film *The Remains of the Day*. Emma Thompson, who plays Miss Kenton, the maid, has nursed tender, romantic affection for Anthony Hopkins, Stevens the butler, throughout the movie. Near the end (spoiler coming!) the two of them are alone, late at night, in a hallway of the mansion in which they serve. Miss Kenton, awkwardly and self-consciously, pushes their conversation beyond the usual "good night," even though it's evident that Stevens is too emotionally constipated and stiff to respond in kind. She moves closer, giving him an opportunity to express the affection she hopes he feels—and despite her vulnerability, her willingness at long last to make a fool of herself if that's what it takes, he continues standing stiffly and staring straight ahead. She continues right up to the point beyond which she would lose all self-respect, and finally moves away, sparing herself and Stevens any further embarrassment. Such a painful scene to watch. I have found it impossible to dislike Emma Thompson in any role she has taken since then.

Don't leave your spouse hanging, even if you're tired and cranky like Anthony Hopkins. Kiss back. Hug back. And like it.

Habits of Life

These are the habits that work well not only in marriage but also in every other relationship. They're relationship strengtheners.

Be positive. In other words, focus on the positive things about the relationship and about your partner. No one wants to be subjected to a constant diet of negativity.

Talking about the future? Paint a hopeful picture of where your family can be in a year, even if the challenges to make that come true are difficult. You and your spouse both need that hope. "Where there is no vision, the people perish" (Prov. 29:18 KJV).

Talking about your spouse? I can say with confidence that there are things about your spouse that could be improved, just as there are things about you (and definitely me) that could be improved. But in the midst of a crisis is not the time to bring them up. So speak instead of what you love about your spouse, of what you admire, of what about them gives you hope for a better future once you've survived the crisis and moved on.

This is a great principle for life in general. Think how great most workplaces and most sports teams would be if everyone practiced that simple rule: be positive.

Be patient. This may shock you: none of us are perfect. Dave speaking: But wait—does that mean I'm saying my wife, Cindy, isn't perfect? That's easy to answer: she's absolutely perfect for me. And the reason she's perfect for me is because she's not perfect. If she were, I'd be feeling guilty about all of my own imperfections, and they are legion. We can be relaxed and comfortable around each other because we know neither of us is perfect, we're okay with that, and we extend automatic forgiveness toward each other when those imperfections show up.

So when something doesn't get done that was supposed to be done, when someone keeps you waiting, when someone's temper gets the best of them and words are said—be patient. Stuff happens. People get sick, people forget, things break. Be patient. Be forgiving.

What a relief it is when others extend this kindness to us!

Let down your guard. Be vulnerable. Many if not most of us have an overblown and misguided sense of personal dignity. We don't like to look like a fool. When I say it's *misguided,* I mean that our attempts to protect ourselves and our reputation often end up costing us the things we'd most like to keep—like relationships.

You can't connect with someone at a deep, intimate level, whether as lovers or as friends, without letting down your guard and making yourself vulnerable. Do you risk being hurt? Absolutely. Do it anyway. The truth is, we're powerless to protect ourselves against the people we love. The only way to avoid being hurt in relationships is to not have any.

Risk it. Open up. Especially with your spouse. Do what Stevens the butler in *The Remains of the Day* could not.

Be kind. And now at the end of the chapter we've come back to this pivotal concept. *Be kind and compassionate to one another.* That's the best summary I can think of to describe what we've been discussing in this chapter.

Consider the parable of the good Samaritan in Luke 10:30–37:

> Jesus said: "A man was going down from Jerusalem to Jericho, when he was attacked by robbers. They stripped him of his

> clothes, beat him and went away, leaving him half dead. A priest happened to be going down the same road, and when he saw the man, he passed by on the other side. So too, a Levite, when he came to the place and saw him, passed by on the other side. But a Samaritan, as he traveled, came where the man was; and when he saw him, he took pity on him. He went to him and bandaged his wounds, pouring on oil and wine. Then he put the man on his own donkey, brought him to an inn and took care of him. The next day he took out two denarii and gave them to the innkeeper. 'Look after him,' he said, 'and when I return, I will reimburse you for any extra expense you may have.'
>
> "Which of these three do you think was a neighbor to the man who fell into the hands of robbers?"
>
> The expert in the law replied, "The one who had mercy on him."
>
> Jesus told him, "Go and do likewise."

Wonderful story. But notice something in particular: Throughout Jesus's story, the Samaritan doesn't say a single word to the injured man. He speaks to the innkeeper, but the story includes no words exchanged between the Samaritan and the man injured by robbers. The emphasis, throughout, is on the acts of service the Samaritan performed for the injured man out of kindness.

Go and do likewise—sometimes accompanied by words, and sometimes in articulate silence.

Discussion Questions
for Couples and Small Groups

1. What one concept in this chapter most challenged your thinking?
2. There's a list of thoughtful gestures on pages 126–28. Is there one of those that has particularly blessed you when your spouse extended that thoughtful gesture toward you?
3. In the story of the good Samaritan in Luke 10:30–37, the Samaritan was kind toward the injured man without speaking to him, as far as we know. What acts of kindness has your spouse shown you without using words—in "articulate silence"?
4. The five love languages identified by Gary Chapman in *The 5 Love Languages* are words of affirmation, quality time, receiving gifts, acts of service, and physical touch. Which of the five is your love language that most speaks love to you when exercised by others? Which of the five is the one you find it easiest to express? Which of the five is your spouse's love language?

CHAPTER 7

The Power of Serving While Suffering

> If each of us were to list both the best and worst things that have ever happened to us, we are bound to see overlap in the two lists. . . . God has used some of the worst things to accomplish some of the best. . . . Someday, we will see how it was true all along—each time suffering came along.
>
> —Randy Alcorn

Carol and I (Gene) had a big decision to make. Just a year before we received the heart-wrenching news of our son's arrest, I had left my career in the insurance industry to work side by side with my wife in ministry. I sold my business and moved from my downtown office building to a makeshift workspace in our basement. From there I managed Carol's speaking contracts, ordered and shipped her books, made flight arrangements, and worked with meeting planners all over the country. Ministry was our only income. *What would we do now?*

Overwhelmed with grief, fear, and questions, we were unable to think clearly about what we would be doing for the next minute—let alone how we would pay for our son's defense, make our next mortgage payment, put food on the table, and survive in unthinkable circumstances. Carol's next speaking engagement was in five days—we would be driving to a conference center in Ohio. We depleted our retirement funds to pay the deposit for an attorney, with the promise that we would send monthly checks to take care of the remainder of his fee—and those checks would be more than our mortgage payments! We urgently needed income. If at all possible, Carol needed to keep speaking, regardless of how emotionally depleted she might feel with our son facing imprisonment.

It was a four-hour trip by car to the Ohio location, and we dreaded arriving. As we drove, Carol intermittently wept. I wondered: *Despite our financial need, is it even possible to continue this kind of ministry during such a devastating family crisis? Should we quit public ministry?*

We arrived. I unloaded the car while Carol had a quick dinner with the worship leader before the weekend conference began.

Carol picks up the story:

Amy and I sat at a small table at the back of the dining area. Midway through the meal, she said, "I almost canceled my commitment to lead worship at this event. My husband and I are in full-time music ministry, and we're not making it financially. We're about to lose our house. We're declaring bankruptcy. After all our years of serving the Lord, it feels like he's been unfair to us. I can't tell my children God is faithful."

My eyes flooded with tears. I put my hand over Amy's and blurted: "I understand. My husband and I are in the middle of a gigantic family crisis. It's not our marriage, but it's huge—and I don't know if I can stand up on that platform and speak. We will be two broken people ministering in incredible pain." We held each other, wept, and prayed together before making our way to the meeting room.

Amy led powerful worship songs, and I sobbed through each one. Then I was introduced, and I didn't know if I'd be able to make it through my presentation without falling apart emotionally in front of hundreds of women. Bible in hand, I stepped onto the platform and opened God's Word. At first, I felt as if I was on autopilot, saying what seemed appropriate based on past experience. But about ten minutes into the message, everything changed—I sensed an empowerment that I can only explain in the supernatural dimension. I changed the direction of my presentation, departed from what I'd planned to say, and spoke spontaneously from the fullness of my broken heart. As God's truth poured from my mouth, I felt as if I were stomping on the enemy shouting, *You lose! You meant to wipe the parents out along with their child, but you're failing. You're already defeated. We're* not *quitting! We're* not *giving up on God!*

Was it the best presentation I've ever given? No. But it was honest, raw, and real. I didn't share the story of our journey with our son—it was not yet time for that. But I spoke with more emotion, compassion, and heartfelt spiritual fervor than I ever had before. I had desperately needed Jesus to come through for me—and he did! He did for Amy too. From that point forward, no matter what was going on with our son's case, I knew I could stand up and speak about the God of all comfort. In serving others, my own heart was reminded of biblical truth, and I was encouraged and blessed in the process.

When Suffering Comes

When painful circumstances enter our marriages, we often struggle with questions:

- Why would a loving God allow such a terrible thing to happen to us when we've tried to be faithful to him?
- Why does God allow suffering to come to some couples but not others?
- How can what's happened to our family ever work out for our good and for God's glory?
- Why do some people get answers to their prayers for healing, for restoration, for financial relief, or for an easier life—but our prayers get none?

With no easy answers, we get up each day and take care of the urgency our situation demands—holding on until our head hits the pillow at night—and then we start over again when the alarm goes off the next morning. We echo Job with this thought: "If my misery could be weighed and my troubles be put on the scales, they would outweigh all the sands of the sea" (Job 6:2–3 NLT). We're often tempted to withdraw from public life and ministry for a variety of reasons—but mostly because we're exhausted from dealing with our situation and sometimes because we're disappointed in God.

Jack and Lael Arrington's Story

Lael starts the story:

> Even before we left for the mission field in Costa Rica, my feet were becoming sore. And once we arrived there, it became worse. I suspected that was due to the tension of driving eight-hour days along "highways" only a few yards wide with 600-foot drop-offs and potholes the size of hot tubs; it was making my knees and hips ache too. But two weeks after we arrived in Costa Rica, I was diagnosed with rheumatoid arthritis.
>
> My descent from slightly tarnished high-school beauty queen to cripple was swift. All my dreams leaked out of my heart and left a barren grief that occasionally trickled down my cheeks as I passed certain signposts—the days I could no longer play my guitar for a gospel outreach event or wear my wedding ring—the little swollen, aching things that stood for the big broken thing.
>
> Fatigue was constant, but I dreaded going to bed. The weight of the bedsheet on my toes felt like the dentist's lead X-ray vest. I would want to turn on my side for relief, but to push on my swollen joints to make it happen was like choosing a brief flogging. The inflammation and pain so weakened me that my walking slowed to a shuffle. I couldn't stand up from a chair without Jack's help.
>
> Psalm 94:17 says, "Unless the Lord had given me help, I would soon have dwelt in the silence of death." As I spiraled into a black hole of pain and loss, I knew God's sovereign

protection and love surrounded us, but if Jack had not stepped up to console me and physically help me, my struggle with self-care and mobility would have sent me into the depths. He was truly "Jesus with skin on" to me.

He helped me get dressed when the pain of reaching to the floor to pull up pants was excruciating.

He helped me comb the back of my hair that I could no longer reach.

While the rest of the group (or the world) walked at a normal pace, he learned to slow down without complaining in order to not leave me and my shuffle behind.

He lifted me out of low chairs and into high car seats.

He lent me his arm and his strength to navigate stairs.

He chauffeured me everywhere, including to the doctor who informed us that we were expecting a longed-for baby—a ray of light and hope in such a dark time.

Even so, the pregnancy did complicate my care. Two and a half months after arriving in Costa Rica I bought a ticket to return to the US full of questions and concerns for my doctors there.

I boarded the plane and my aching body collapsed into my seat, fighting back tears—and mostly winning until I saw Jack. Somehow, he had found a place to park by the end of the runway. As my plane roared past, he stood at the airport fence, waving and waving and blowing kisses.

I think I wept as we flew over all of Nicaragua and maybe even Honduras. To the pain, cracked self-image, broken dreams, and raging first trimester hormones I was already experiencing, I now added a profound sense of aloneness. Just when I needed Jack the most, I was putting six hundred miles an hour between us.

Doctors in the US recommended that we return to the States, so Jack packed up all our belongings and headed north to the US.

Jack picks up the story:

Driving through Mexico, the rain and wind began to blot out the road. I crept along until there *was* no road. Only a giant washout fifty feet across. I was in the middle of a hurricane. Drenched, brokenhearted, and angry at God, I returned to the previous town.

I sat at a table in a small café, my heart churning. How would I make it to Lael in Texas?

A man approached and asked, "Are you a missionary?"

Though I didn't much feel like one at that moment, I said, "Yes."

The man said, "Would you tell me and my family about Jesus?"

Wow. It was as if for a moment God parted the curtains of his hidden, sovereign will to let me know he hadn't forgotten me, and that things were working according to his plan. After I'd told the man and his family—who were in a shot-up van trying to flee El Salvador to find a new life—about Jesus, he told me he had discovered a better way out of town.

Lael continues:

In that encounter, God was reaffirming to Jack that the way through suffering was serving—laying aside his own anger and hurt and reaching out to share God's love with this refugee family.

Jack couldn't wait to share the story with me as soon as he made it to Texas. Our joy that God was still using us, even though my rheumatoid arthritis had vaporized our dreams of serving in Central America, was a beautiful banner of love over the road ahead—though we didn't know where that road would lead. It drew us together and moved us into the next chapter God was opening for us.[1]

Rediscovering Your Joy

One of the most powerful lessons Carol and I (Gene) have learned on our journey with our son is that God has given us a ministry to other people who are going through the same or similar experiences. This is, I think, the most important point in this chapter, and remember this if you remember nothing else: God will give you people to serve while you are suffering—and when you accept those opportunities, a deep, extravagant joy will replace discouragement and self-pity. Our author friend Kathe Wunnenberg writes: "Sometimes we go through what we go through, to help others go through what we went through."[2]

In Genesis we read about the unfair treatment of Joseph—and not only when his brothers sold him into slavery. Later, while he was working as the most trusted servant in the home of Potiphar, he refused the sexual advances of Mrs. Potiphar and wound up in prison—for many years—all while he was innocent of any wrongdoing!

> But while Joseph was there in the prison, the LORD was with him; he showed him kindness and granted him favor in the eyes of the prison warden. So the warden put Joseph in charge of all those held in the prison and he was made responsible for all that was done there. The warden paid no attention to anything under Joseph's care, because the LORD was with Joseph and gave him success in whatever he did. (Gen. 39:20–23)

After this, the Egyptian pharaoh became so offended by his chief cupbearer and head baker that he put them in custody in the house of the captain of the guard in the prison where Joseph was incarcerated. The captain of the guard assigned Joseph to them, and he became their personal attendant.

Later in the story, we discover that these two jailbirds held the key to the eventual release of Joseph. But first, Joseph had to look beyond his own misery and serve these men. They had dreams—and dreams were Joseph's specialty. He interpreted the dreams of both men, using the gift God had given him to help others. Instead of wallowing in self-pity, Joseph took time to serve two of his fellow inmates. The result? God opened the door for him to be promoted to a place of honor and eventually into the top level of leadership in Egypt. (Read the whole story in Genesis 40–41.) He served while suffering, and God blessed him.

We rediscover our joy as we fully engage in helping others who are sometimes in a worse situation than we are. Serving others changes our perspective.

Dirk and Harriet Buursma's Story

Young couples approaching the birth of their first child seldom think, *This child will be born with extreme disabilities, and our lives will never be the same from that moment on.* Instead, most couples, giddily optimistic, are thinking ahead to showing their child off to friends and family and strangers in the grocery store, to T-ball games and ballet classes and valedictorian speeches and father/daughter dances at weddings. But for many couples, those dreams will have to wait for future children.

Dirk Buursma says:

It became clear right out of the gate that our firstborn son, Paul's, condition was serious. He was born acutely ill—babies born with his condition at that time had a 98 percent mortality rate. He first had to undergo emergency surgery within hours of his birth to correct a diaphragmatic hernia and was then flown by helicopter to Ann Arbor, Michigan, to be given ECMO—extracorporeal membrane oxygenation—considered an experimental treatment at the time.

Dirk's wife, Harriet, observes:

I'll never forget us praying during those long hours that night as he was being flown to Ann Arbor and then undergoing treatment that God would spare him. Of course, our prayers started out with bargaining, pointing out to God that both Dirk and I had grown up in Christian homes and that we were dedicated to serving him. We couldn't understand what God was doing. Why was this happening to us?

And yet by the end of those long hours of prayer, we came to this conclusion: "God, he is your child. Do with him as you will."

Dirk:

We had Paul with us for thirty-two years. Yes, he faced significant challenges because of his cerebral palsy and had nearly constant physical needs. But our daily experience with Paul was that God had an amazing purpose for his life—and for our lives. I can't imagine someone more empathetic, more caring.

He taught us things we would not know today if we hadn't had him for those thirty-two years. Despite the struggles, the waking up every two hours in the night to check on him and turn him so he could breathe more easily, we so often thought back to that night of wrestling with God and said to each other, "This is what *God* chose for Paul."

Paul was our beautiful child. He was who he was—a deeply loved child of God and our gift from above—and so we just had to learn to adjust to whatever came our way day by day and to not look too far ahead. As life went on, though we were reminded of some of the things we knew we would *not* be experiencing with Paul, we also knew that we were being taught lessons that many parents don't get to experience with their children.

Harriet:

Every year on his birthday, I would have a "come-to-Jesus moment" and all of a sudden be struggling again. We experienced those moments throughout his life, and for me it had to do with the milestones. We celebrated his sixteenth birthday, and I was suddenly reminded that, unlike most teenagers, he's not going to be asking for the car keys. Or climbing mountains on a family vacation.

Dirk:

As his parents, sure, we would have loved for him to be able to walk. But his smile lit up a room, and his sense of humor kept us laughing. And he could talk, he could sing, he could pray like you wouldn't believe. He was a prayer warrior who always let others know he would be talking to God about their needs.

> Having Paul changed our perspective about what's important in life. Others sometimes said, "Wow, that's such a burden. We feel sorry for you—your responsibilities in caring for your son don't allow you to do this or that." But life with Paul was a gift to us, beyond my ability to express—the things we learned, the people we became through the experience. He constantly pointed us to God and to our need to depend on God in all things, to show that in our weakness, we can find our strength in God.
>
> Life with Paul made us more aware of what's truly important. It made us aware that life is fragile. It made us more aware of the needs around us, of the joy to be found in looking outside oneself, in learning how to serve others in love.

Paul Buursma died in December 2015. Throughout much of his life, he and his family had been involved in the Christian ministry Joni & Friends, founded by Joni Eareckson Tada. With Joni's example before them of someone who finds joy in serving while suffering, it's natural that Dirk and Harriet began, in their sense of grief and loss after their son's death, to think of ways to turn that loss into opportunities to serve. And one obvious way was this: Over the years, they had invested in a number of pieces of equipment necessary for Paul to experience life to the fullest—a manual wheelchair, a special-needs bike carrier, an adult-size racing stroller, and so on. What better way to serve families whose situations are similar to theirs but who have limited resources than by donating that equipment to them?

One of the special ministries of Joni & Friends is Wheels for the World, which makes wheelchairs available to individuals with disabilities around the world. Dirk and Harriet offered to make Paul's wheelchair available for donation, and they were able to go along on a trip to Peru to meet the recipient.

"We felt like the least qualified members of the team," Dirk laughs. "Speaking for myself anyway—I'm not a therapist. And I'm *surely* not a mechanic. And yet here we were, joining this wonderful, incredibly gifted team. We saw ourselves as the encouragers. The cheerleaders. 'Go team!'"

After a long, involved process—which can only be explained as orchestrated by God from beginning to end—to get the wheelchair delivered from Michigan to Southern California so it could be shipped to Peru, the Buursmas flew out of Chicago with a few other members of the team, made connections in Miami and Lima, and arrived in Chiclayo, Peru's fourth largest city, on a Saturday in October 2016.

Harriet picks up the story:

> So the chairs were going to be distributed in two different churches, one for the first half of the week and one for the second half. When we got to the church where the chairs were being stored, we were eager to find Paul's chair—we had been unable to shake the thought that maybe, just maybe, his chair had been somehow diverted or inadvertently left behind and wouldn't be here, after all our arrangements. In fact, we had been afraid we would get here and be unable to find it among the many, many other chairs, but we were told it had been shrink-wrapped in red.
>
> We went to the location, and the chairs were stored in the main gathering room and four rooms that had been recently added at the back. Just *crammed* in there. We looked in the first room. No, nothing there. We looked in the second room. Nothing there. Third room—nothing there either, and by this time we're getting nervous! After all, this had been one of our nightmares.

I was the first to go into the last room. Dirk was right behind me. I looked around and didn't see anything at first. We continued carefully scanning the room, and way in the very back corner, we saw a chair wrapped in red—Paul's chair. What an emotional rush! We both wept openly.

We had to move the chairs from that church to the church where the first distribution would take place. The chairs had been grouped by size—twelve inches wide, thirteen, fourteen, fifteen, and so on. There were no trucks, so we had to make several trips back and forth to wheel the chairs by hand the ten blocks or so from one facility to the other. Paul's chair was in the queue to be transported, and I made sure I would be the one to wheel it over. And as I was pushing it along—well, I totally lost it. There I was, pushing his wheelchair along a busy street in Peru. I had pushed that chair so many times with Paul in it, and now we were about to make that same chair available, as an expression of Paul's life and compassion, to a Peruvian child who needed it so badly.

Dirk was up ahead of me, and I called out, "Dirk, come back!" I was having such a powerful emotional experience, I wanted him to share it. So the two of us walked along together, tears in our eyes, in the anticipation of delivering our son's wheelchair to a boy or girl in this faraway land—we had no idea who. I still remember it so vividly.

Dirk continues:

On Monday morning, the forty or so of us on the team gathered for devotions, and one of the team leaders pointed out Paul's chair and told our story—ours and Paul's. And then we all laid hands on the chair and prayed for the person who would receive it. It was a very beautiful moment, very powerful.

Then we all went to the church. Monday came and went. No likely candidate for Paul's chair turned up that day—no one who was the right size or had the right level of disability because Paul's chair, due to his own needs, had everything. Footplates, lumbar support, hip support, head support, and so on. So the prayer of the team was that God would bring just the right person, probably somebody with cerebral palsy like Paul.

Harriet:

I should explain that our Wheels for the World team included people from four different countries, including a group of translators from Ecuador. All of the families needing wheelchairs spoke only Spanish, and many of us on the team spoke no Spanish. In the church we were in, there were six stations set up, each with a physical therapist and at least two mechanics, so that we could work with six potential recipients at a time. Two of those stations were manned by people from Ecuador, so language was not a problem, but the other four included a translator. When each family entered the station, the therapist would ask specific questions: "What is your disabling condition? How long have you needed a wheelchair? Where will you use your chair?" Then we asked permission to pray with that family, and when they granted that permission, we prayed with them, asking for God's blessing on the family and for God to lead us to just the right wheelchair for that individual. The whole process was bathed in prayer.

Dirk:

So on Tuesday, same thing as Monday—there was no good fit for Paul's chair. Wednesday was a day for cultural activities. Wednesday night, at the hotel, I had a very restless night: *We came all the way from Grand Rapids, Michigan, to Peru to give this chair to someone, and two days have come and gone and nothing's happened!* At about one in the morning, I suddenly had a sense of God communicating to me that this was all happening in his time, according to his timetable—that he had it under control. And that was enough—I was able to fall asleep for a while.

Thursday morning, I got to the church before all the activity started and had a time of prayer, first by myself in the storage room where Paul's chair was located, and then with the entire team. Around the middle of the morning, I thought I'd go check on Paul's chair, so I headed to the room where the chairs were stored. Paul's chair wasn't there. So I raced over to the sanctuary where all the stations were set up, and there was Paul's chair at one of the stations, and one of the therapists was working on it.

Harriet was already there, and she was quick to tell me, "Now, remember, we're testing this out. It's not a sure thing yet." She wanted to make sure I didn't get too excited, because the young man they were testing with the chair, Aldair, twelve years old—a precious kid—was very slender and much shorter than Paul. Still I had a strong sense that prayers were being answered and that this young man just might be the person!

Harriet:

At two o'clock, we were still all there, still going. Aldair's mom and aunt—his mom's sister—were there with him. We were gathered around them, but of course they spoke only Spanish and we couldn't communicate with them, which was so frustrating! But it's amazing what you can communicate without words—just through body language and smiles. Throughout the process, we could tell by the nods and the laughter and the broad grins that Aldair's mom and aunt were so excited about the beautiful chair that was being so lovingly prepared for Aldair.

Poor Aldair was in a lot of pain. He was very spastic, very rigid. His mom was standing behind him, trying to hold his head straight because he tended to tilt to the side. At one point she had to take him to the bathroom—she had to carry him. He attended a special school, but because of his needs she had to be there with him each day. So she couldn't have a job.

Dirk:

So the afternoon wore on. Three o'clock, and they still weren't done. It was five o'clock that day before Aldair and his family finally left with what had been Paul's wheelchair and was now Aldair's. It took that long to modify it to make sure everything was just right. Every piece of that chair had to be adjusted. They had to drill new holes in the back, change the height of the footplates—it was just an exhausting day for all involved.

We took a whole series of pictures with the family as they were getting ready to leave. We were all tired and emotionally spent, but we were all filled with amazement at what God had just done. A part of Paul's life experience, his legacy, now resides with a young man in Peru, and we will always be connected with Aldair and his precious family.

And so with tears in our eyes, we watched them wheel Aldair down the very narrow sidewalk along the narrow street toward the transportation that would take them to their home and to their new situation. We were so relieved and grateful to have accomplished the one thing that we had come to do. We felt such incredible joy and peace!

Harriet:

Can I leave you with one last Paul story that illustrates why this use of his chair was so fitting? At his memorial service,

Calvin College's chaplain, Pastor Mary, shared some of the conversations she had with Paul when he got to know her during his time in a special program at Calvin. In one of their last conversations, as his health was deteriorating, Paul asked her, "Do you know what heaven's going to be like?" As she considered how to answer, she was thinking, *I know where he's headed with this. He's been in a wheelchair his whole life. He'll start with the words, "Am I going to be able to"—and then he'll ask if he'll be able to walk, if he'll be able to run. And I'm so happy to tell him that he will.* So she gave Paul some insight into her view of what heaven will be like. Paul listened and then said, "I was just wondering—in heaven, will I be able to kneel?"

And that is reflective of the thirty-two years we had with Paul. He taught us how important it is to always be on our knees, in body or in spirit, saying, "I can't figure this out, God, and I don't have the wisdom or the strength to get through it anyway. So I'm just going to trust you, because I know that you've got this." And he does—God's got it. We don't. We don't know what to do with what faces us in life, any more than the young couple we were when Paul was born knew how to rise to that challenge. We didn't know how to fix it. But God did. When you face things that just don't seem humanly possible, you do it as a couple, always seeking God's best for yourselves and your loved ones. And you learn—you learn to laugh when you should be crying.

Practical Truth

Pastor Tim Keller writes, "Suffering is unbearable if you aren't certain that God is for you and with you."[3] When you encounter unthinkable or difficult challenges as a married couple, even in your pain look for ways to serve others, for these reasons:

- Serving others allows us to partner with God. "The LORD is on my side; I will not fear" (Ps. 118:6 NKJV).
- Serving others produces blessing. "Give away your life; you'll find life given back, but not merely given back—given back with bonus and blessing. Giving, not getting, is the way. Generosity begets generosity" (Luke 6:38 MSG).
- Serving others brings glory to God. "Do you have the gift of helping others? Do it with all the strength and energy that God supplies. Then everything you do will bring glory to God through Jesus Christ" (1 Pet. 4:11 NLT).
- Serving others shifts our focus off our own challenges and onto someone else. It makes us Jesus-focused. "And the King will say, 'I tell you the truth, when you did it to one of the least of these my brothers and sisters, you were doing it to me!'" (Matt. 25:40 NLT).

In addition to all of these biblical truths, serving others brings better health and mental well-being. The Mental Health Foundation reports: "Doing things for others helps maintain good health. Positive emotions reduce stress and boost our immune system, and in turn can protect us against disease."[4] Serving others is good for us physically and spiritually.

Carol writes: For a while, my own grief over the incarceration of my son kept me self-focused. My thoughts swirled around fear of the future; I stressed over trying to make sure my son was safe, and I was anxious about what others might think of our family. Eventually, an important change took place, and I remember just when. We were standing in line with other families waiting to go through security at the prison. We spoke to those around us and met lonely wives and children who had been separated from their husbands and fathers due to incarceration. We met inmates who needed Bible studies and reading material. We noticed that the visitation room was short on items that children could use to do activities with their incarcerated parent during their visits. Gene and I launched the nonprofit organization Speak Up for Hope (www.SpeakUpforHope.org), which benefits inmates and their families. Friends of this ministry donate thousands of dollars each year so we can provide inmates with excellent reading material, postage, electronic tablets, care packages, and greeting cards to send to their family members. Wives and moms of inmates receive Boxes of Hope that contain comfort items for women, along with a letter assuring them of our prayers. We're able to place games, coloring books, and crayons in the visitation areas of prisons so children have something fun to do with their incarcerated parent when they come for visits. We began collecting donations toward the Boxes of Hope project for wives and moms of inmates. Other people collected games for the prison visitation rooms, and many donated toward Bible study books.

One day while doing the laundry, I noticed that Gene's pile of black T-shirts was shorter than usual. When I asked him what was happening to his T-shirts, he said, "You'll find out soon enough."

The following weekend we were standing in line at the prison, waiting to get through security. A new guideline had been put in place for the visitation area: Women were no longer allowed to wear sleeveless shirts or blouses. I looked up and noticed that a woman who had already waited for over two hours to make it to the front of the line had been turned away—she was wearing a sleeveless blouse. She was sobbing.

I suddenly realized that Gene was no longer standing next to me. I looked around and spotted him in the parking lot, apparently returning from our car. He was carrying a black T-shirt. (I hadn't noticed the supply of black T-shirts Gene had been carrying in his trunk because often, due to work and ministry schedules, Gene and I drove to the prison separately.) He approached the woman and said, "Here, put this on and go back to the front of the line. It's my gift to you today. Have a wonderful visit with your family."

He returned to my side in the line of people waiting to visit their inmate loved ones. I said, "So *that's* what's been happening to your T-shirts!"

He smiled and said, "It's my ministry."

Ever since the day I found out about Gene's T-shirt ministry, we've been working together to pass them out to visitors who need them in order to pass inspection. The more we continue to serve others together, the less we focus on our own loss. As we invest in the lives of others, God doubles our joy.

Final Thoughts

Remember Jack and Lael Arrington? They returned to the States following Lael's debilitating diagnosis of rheumatoid arthritis. But God faithfully met their needs—physically, emotionally, spiritually, and financially—in remarkable ways as they have continued to serve others during the past three decades in local church ministry and through Lael's written and spoken words.

Lael says, "God writes the most amazing stories on the pages of our lives. High drama. Great stakes. His signature on his redemptive work is most clear when he blasts through insurmountable walls with last-second timing. More glory for him. More joy for us. Our hearts echo the praises of Psalm 107:1: 'Give thanks to the LORD, for he is good; his love endures forever.'"

Billy Graham vividly reminds us of another important truth. "All around you are people whose lives are filled with trouble and sorrow, and they need your compassion and encouragement."[5] There is power in serving while suffering—for the receivers and for the givers. Give it a try. You'll like it!

Discussion Questions
for Couples and Small Groups

1. What was your main take-away from this chapter?
2. Has there been a situation in your life that was both the best and the worst thing that ever happened to you? Explain.

3. Near the end of his life, Paul Buursma, a prayer warrior with severe cerebral palsy, confined to a wheelchair, wanted to know whether in heaven he would be able not to run, not to dance, but to kneel. Despite his own discomfort and his own limitations, his mind was on service. When have you witnessed others with that same ability and willingness to transcend their own suffering for the sake of serving God or others?
4. Name a time when you were suffering and someone served you. What did they do? What did it mean to you?
5. "Give away your life; you'll find life given back, but not merely given back—given back with bonus and blessing. Giving, not getting, is the way. Generosity begets generosity" (Luke 6:38 MSG). In what ways have you received more than you've given when you've served others?

CHAPTER 8

Divine Surprises

> When we lose one blessing, another is often most unexpectedly given in its place.
>
> —C. S. Lewis

I (Carol) like predictability. It's not that I don't enjoy an occasional surprise, but overall I like to make my to-do list and have a reasonable expectation about how my day, week, or month will unfold. I also like to know I've gotten important tasks done during the day. If I accomplish something of merit that isn't on my list, I add it to the list at the end of the day (after finishing the task) in order to get the personal thrill of drawing a line through it.

For people like me, an unexpected crisis or a long-term interruption in my carefully spelled-out plans feels like an unwanted intrusion. It can put me on edge, making me antsy, critical, exasperated, frustrated, and irritable. That can make wives with my personality type not much fun to live with! (Ask Gene Kent.)

When our son was arrested and eventually sentenced to life without parole, I would have never imagined that there could be a hidden blessing in that harsh reality. This was not just an interruption—this was a life-altering, marriage-testing, flat-out-horrific event from which we might never recover—as a family and as a couple.

Jason's arrest was not just a surprise but a shock—and even that is understating its effect. Before we received that fateful phone call, if I'd been asked to write down one hundred possible scenarios I might someday face in my life, my son's arrest for murder would not have been on that list. It was too impossible, too horrific, too unimaginable, and too out of character.

The word *surprise* can be used as either a noun or a verb and carries two paradoxical meanings. The verb form of the word means to startle, stun, flabbergast, stagger, shock, stupefy (to leave open-mouthed), dumbfound, daze, bewilder, jolt, or shake up. Yes, indeed! Gene and I experienced the entirety of that emotional roller coaster. (More about the second definition of *surprise* later.)

Dealing with the Unexpected

This book is filled with examples of times when an unexpected crisis comes into our reasonably content lives and threatens to destroy, or at least erode, our happiness as married couples. And of course such developments always come at an inappropriate and inconvenient time, often causing collateral damage along the way, negatively impacting the married couple, the family, and sometimes friends close enough to observe what's happening.

The unexpected nature of this type of surprise doesn't allow for advance planning or prevention. It hits suddenly and without warning, wreaking havoc with emotions, finances, daily routines, careers, and future goals. It's devastating!

The Trial of Their Lives

Janet and Craig McHenry live a half mile from their ranch in the Sierra Valley in northern California. Janet is an award-winning speaker and the author of twenty-four books. Craig was a lawyer, but he started farming in 1985, gradually acquiring land and cattle. Eventually he transitioned into full-time ranching.

Janet writes:

> In May 2005 my husband was convicted of six felony counts of animal abuse relating to the deaths of six calves and an old bull on our ranch in the Sierra Valley. The calves had bedded down with the old bull in a dry creek bed during a two-day blizzard in 2001 that covered them with snow. Two weeks later the snow melted, and a disgruntled neighbor, who had continually harassed Craig over the years because Craig would not sell him a strip of land, called the local animal control officer. Charges were filed.

Four Years Later

The case finally went to trial, but the judge seemed to have it in for Craig from the start. He mocked defense witnesses, including two beef cattle veterinarians and Janet.

While Janet testified that Craig cared about his newborn calves so much that he brought them into their home to warm them during harsh conditions, the judge interrupted her comment.

Janet continues:

> The judge refused to allow the admission of evidence such as auction records that would have shown Craig had gotten excellent prices for his cattle before and after the incident. The judge also refused to allow testimony from the defense's chief witness, a professor at the UC Davis School of Veterinary Medicine who would have testified that the necropsy report showed that the two dead animals tested had died well fed.

The Trial and Its Aftermath

Janet and Craig's marriage had gone through its ups and downs over the years. When working in Craig's law office ten years earlier, Janet even typed up a Dissolution of Marriage Petition, "just to see what it would look like." Their commitment to their four children kept them together over the years, but Craig's trial was particularly hard on Janet, who felt Craig "should have, could have done something to make it all go away." Both of them believed that as difficult as the trial was, in the end he would be acquitted—after all, he wasn't actually guilty of anything—and all would be forgotten.

Craig was convicted.

The conviction was particularly hurtful for Janet, since one of the jurors was the business manager for the small school district for which Janet worked, one was a substitute teacher who had subbed for her, and one, the head juror, was the son of a woman with whom she prayerwalked.

Janet continued:

> We were fearful of the ramifications of the conviction. Craig's cattle could have been taken away. He would no longer be able to practice law—something he had not done for a decade since he began ranching full-time, but it was still something that could have helped the family income in the future. And he had just finished the coursework and passed the exams for his doctorate; he had wanted to teach political science at the college level, but a conviction would prevent that.

The sentencing hearing took place the same month Janet's book *PrayerStreaming: Staying in Touch with God All Day Long*[1] was released. She *did* pray continually—as a mom, as a wife, as a high school English teacher, and as a prayerwalker for her community in the Sierra Valley. "Our county only has about three thousand people—and no stoplights," Janet said. "Everyone knows everyone."

They had waited two months for the sentencing hearing, and the courthouse was packed that day with family and friends of Janet and Craig, including six pastors. "The judge seemed startled," Janet said. "The room was clearly full of people who loved and supported us. And letters testifying to Craig's character had come from the superintendent of schools and many others locally respected."

In spite of the support, Craig was sentenced to four years of probation and a fine of more than $10,000. Unable to leave the state of California, they even had to get permission to attend their church in nearby Reno, Nevada.

"It was ironic," Janet said. "Supposedly, he was starving his cattle, but they didn't take his cattle away."

Janet didn't know there would be much more to this story in the future.

Sweetest Surprises

Sometimes in the middle of our greatest crises in marriage God gives us sweet surprises along the way. We may not get the big answer to prayer that we were looking for, but he gives us unexpected splashes of joy that remind us that we're not forgotten. We're reminded of just that in his Word.

Reading Scripture reminds us that God is a God of surprises. Jesus often surprised his followers, and he wants to continue to surprise us with renewed hope and fresh faith. A seldom-quoted verse is Deuteronomy 28:2 (NASB), which reminds us that if we keep God in first place, if we walk in his ways, "all these blessings will . . . overtake [us]." Check out the background of this passage:

- *To whom it's written*: Israel (the new generation entering the promised land)

  Keep in mind that these people, including couples and their families, had been through tough circumstances. They needed to stay focused or they might miss getting into the land God had promised them.
- *The setting*: The east side of the Jordan River, in view of Canaan

Sometimes the hardest part of what we go through is that we're in sight of all of the possibilities of a more stable, comfortable, stress-free marriage, but it doesn't seem likely that we'll ever get there.

- *The author*: Moses
- *The purpose*: To remind the people of what God had done in the past and to encourage them to rededicate their lives to him

One of the sweetest surprises Gene and I have had on our journey with our son is that when we stay tuned in to the faithfulness of God, we are always amazed at his provision. Moses reminded the people: "Know therefore that the LORD your God is God; he is the faithful God, keeping his covenant of love to a thousand generations of those who love him and keep his commands" (Deut. 7:9).

After wandering around for forty years, the old generation died in the desert. They escaped Egypt but never knew the promised land. In this passage in Deuteronomy, Moses is meeting with the sons and daughters of that faithless generation and reminding them of God's contract with his people. The lesson is clear—because of what God had done in the past, Israel should have hope for the future. They should love God completely, listen to instruction, and obey. Moses reminded them that learning these lessons would prepare them to possess the promised land.

Craig and Janet never lost their faith in God. They didn't understand why God allowed such a terrible thing to happen to them, but they continued to believe he is a good and faithful God. They had no idea of the surprises that lay ahead of them.

Surprise Blessings

After the sentencing hearing, Janet's and Craig's friends gathered around them outside the courthouse in little Downieville, an old mining town of a few hundred nestled in the northern Sierras.

Janet was stunned at people's reactions:

- One person said she was so impressed with Craig's faith and with the quiet peace on his face.
- Another said, "He's a living testimony to the power of God."
- Janet's mother said, "He could run for mayor and win!" Even though, as his mother-in-law, she may be prejudiced, she may also have been right: the pages of the local newspaper had been filled for two months with support for Craig and Janet.

Janet turned and looked at her husband with new eyes. He *was* different. The trial had brought out a fortitude and strength she had never noticed before. The man she had married had become a man of faith, a man of God. And she determined at that moment that their marriage would not crumble from the trial or any other challenge that lay ahead.

Over the next two years, they drew strength from God and from each other. In circumstances that would have driven many couples apart, Janet and Craig's marriage grew not weaker but stronger.

Being Caught by Surprise

Remember the verse a few pages ago that reminded us that if we keep God in first place, if we walk in his ways, "all these blessings will . . . overtake [us]" (Deut. 28:2 NASB)? The word *overtake* in Hebrew also carries the meaning "to catch by surprise." If we meditate on the fact that God wants to bless us, that he is continuously good to his children, we'll realize that he wants to surprise us. He wants us to be amazed at the blessings he places in our lives.

The key is to trust him and rely on him as we face our challenges. In the case of Craig and Janet, those challenges were false accusations, loss of reputation, and financial hardship. As we begin to relax and wait on the Lord, our outlook changes and our attitudes are adjusted as we're surprised by his goodness. We develop a daily spirit of anticipation, and we wake up saying, "I can't wait to see what God is going to do today!"

Making a List

When I (Gene) look back on the past two decades of our lives, there's a lot to be sad about. Our only child, arrested at age twenty-five, is now in his forties, and he's still behind bars. His marriage eventually ended in divorce, despite his huge effort to save the relationship. Two beautiful stepdaughters whom Jason had looked forward to raising with his wife are now grown and well into adulthood.

In truth, the past two decades have brought heartache upon heartache. Loss upon loss. Hopes dashed. Efforts to seek an eventual end-of-sentence date through the clemency process have resulted in rejection. Humanly speaking, the threat of despair looms overhead like a big, immovable cloud. So—where can Carol and I find the joy, the hope, and the prospects for a happy marriage when such a big part of our lives is wrapped in so much sorrow?

In order for us to make it, we have to focus on the way God continues to surprise us with his blessings, even in the midst of tragedy, grief, and loss. For a while we were very intermittent about reading the Bible together; we did it separately, but we weren't good about making time every day to read God's Word as a couple. When we did, we found great encouragement in Lamentations 3:22–23 (NLT): "The faithful love of the LORD never ends! His mercies never cease. Great is his faithfulness; his mercies begin afresh each morning."

As we intentionally carved time out of our day to read the Bible together, we also started a list of surprising blessings we'd received over the almost two decades of our son's incarceration. God was always faithful, and we realized his mercies didn't stop. As certainly as the sun rose each day, God brought us new opportunities to bless other people and to receive blessings from them as well.

We started a list, adding to it daily, that included some of the following divine surprises:

- Jason's ministry inside the prison walls flourished. He has taken more than seven hundred inmates through

Dave Ramsey's Financial Peace University class, teaching them how to make out a budget and balance their checkbooks.

- Our son became president of the Gavel Club (an extension of Toastmasters International), helping fellow prisoners to develop their communication skills.
- Jason led men to Christ and mentored them in their walk with the Lord.
- Carol's speaking ministry flourished. The more open we were about telling our story, the more people came to us and shared their own journeys of the unexpected crises that had hit their marriages and their families. We found that those couples who had an incarcerated loved one, instead of hiding in shame, began opening up and talking to us and to others about their struggles and their victories.
- Jason works with me (Gene) to identify inmates who no longer have any outside support. Through the approved Department of Corrections vendors, I'm able to supply those inmates with personal hygiene items, sneakers, socks, workout clothes, and books needed for their classes.
- Friends and family members provided long-term support by visiting our son behind bars, sending us notes of encouragement, and praying for us.
- We launched Speak Up for Hope. If it hadn't been for Jason's arrest and conviction, we're fairly certain this outreach would not have been a part of our lives.
- Once a month, Carol and I are featured on *Homekeepers*, a Christian Television Network program where

> we are interviewed about how churches, communities, and individuals can support jail and prison ministries.

Did we *want* to have such a devastating thing as Jason's arrest and conviction happen to our family? Would we have chosen a severe stress of this nature and the challenges it created in our marriage as well as the financial strain of the trial and the multitude of additional funds needed for a son who is incarcerated? A thousand times no to all of that!

But God, the one who sees the end from the beginning, has surprised us by turning our greatest sorrow into a ministry and an opportunity to help inmates and their families. He surprised us by opening the door for us to bring the needs of prisoners and their loved ones to the forefront on an internationally syndicated television program. He reminded us that our sorrow need never be wasted—instead, it can become a platform upon which we bring hope and healing to others.

And the biggest surprise: We're rediscovering our joy in the middle of a new kind of normal. We're making new friends in the prison visitation line. We're connecting people with the resources they badly need. And we're doing it together, strengthening our marriage in the process.

The Appeal

Nicholas Duncan-Williams, the general overseer of the Action Chapel International ministry, headquartered in Ghana, West Africa, says: "We serve a God of surprises. He is always doing new things with us."

Craig and Janet McHenry can certainly affirm Duncan-Williams's statement. After Craig's sentencing on six felony counts of animal abuse, he and his wife spent a few months resting and recuperating from the exhaustion of the trial. When the court transcripts became available, Janet and Craig spent months examining them and organizing data that showed how the judge had manipulated the case and prejudiced the jury. Together they prepared an appeal with the California Court of Appeals that showed 252 ways the judge had prejudiced the case; they filed it about a year and a half after the trial.

A few months later, Janet and Craig attended a hearing in front of three California Court of Appeals judges in Sacramento. They sat, amazed, as each of the three judges spoke about the case. Janet said: "I remember thinking that they had actually read all of our appeal documents, including the report with all the letters from supporters. They had read the letter from the veterinary school professor. And they saw the injustice."

In the end, the appeals judges overturned the conviction. This cleared Craig's criminal record and required that the county return the fine. However, Janet said, "Clearing your reputation is another thing. I'm sure that there are still people who think Craig is an animal abuser who doesn't know how to take care of his cattle."

Janet and Craig were discovering one of the hard truths about life's unexpected blows: Sometimes they carry inescapable long-term consequences. It's hard to retrieve a good reputation when a personal attack, no matter how inaccurate or unfair, occurs in a community, a church, or your local papers. Even if a retraction is offered, it's usually months later and in small print. What people remember is the drama of the assault on your character, or the hype surrounding an arrest, a conviction, a lawsuit, a harsh accusation. It takes time—sometimes a long time—for people to regain trust.

The Sweet Zone

Craig and Janet McHenry still live in northern California; they still have a cattle ranch in the Sierra Valley. The six years of pain related to the charges against Craig, the trial, and the aftermath could have devastated them and their marriage. But it didn't. They say that now they are enjoying a sweet zone in their lives. Their four kids are married and finished with college, and they have ten grandchildren "so far."

While Janet has retired from teaching, she still is the official scorekeeper for her high school's basketball games, serves on the board of the Sierra Schools Foundation, and most importantly, prayerwalks for her community. And while Craig could have just faded into the woodwork in their town of eight hundred, instead he served four years on the city council and completed fifty-two civil works projects as a volunteer civil works director.

"I remembered," Janet said, "what my mom said the day of the sentencing—that Craig could run for mayor and win. As it turns out, some on the council *did* want him to be mayor, but that wasn't what he wanted to do. He served our little city for four years, quietly doing projects to revitalize it. And I'm so proud of the man of God he is."

An Inventory

Find a few moments of uninterrupted time to read these statements as a couple. Discuss any application they have to your current situation.

- I have been surprised by how hard our journey has been and how many unexpected struggles have come our way.
- At times I feel upset and even angry with God for not protecting us from these circumstances.
- I discovered a good trait in my spouse during our struggle. (Explain what it was.)
- An unexpected blessing I've received is ________________________.
- True or false: Our greatest hardship has become our greatest blessing.

Longing for a Child

Sarah Rollandini is the creator of Infertility Club, a Midwest ministry for women struggling with infertility. She and her husband, Mark, had a deep desire for a child. She shares:

> Life had hummed along according to plan until my husband and I started trying to get pregnant after a few years of marriage—and hit a wall called *infertility*. After a year of trying, we sought diagnosis and treatment. And after all the testing, our doctors came up with a very unsatisfying diagnosis: *unexplained infertility*. And we started down a five-year road of grueling treatments: medication, intrauterine insemination, and in vitro fertilization. During that time, we experienced a tubal pregnancy with twins as well as a

miscarriage. We questioned God's sovereignty in our lives and even in our marriage. Jeremiah's words to the Israelites (29:11 NLT) helped me to hold on to hope even when I was angry and felt abandoned by God: "For I know the plans I have for you," says the LORD. "They are plans for good and not for disaster, to give you a future and a hope."

Our marriage struggled because we had two different ideas of family. My husband, Mark, was fine with just the two of us if it meant we got to hold on to sanity and each other. I couldn't picture my life without children, so there was a lot of conflict over differing goals, as well as over the amount of money we could afford to shell out for treatment.

I remember Mark asking, "Why this obsession with having kids? Am I not enough for you?" But God places a desire for children in the hearts of most women, as he had in mine. Unfortunately, what I saw as a God-given desire, Mark saw as selfishness on my part. Our differences led to years of strain on our relationship. There were times when I thought about giving up on this marriage and starting over. After all, if God wouldn't bless our marriage with children, maybe our marriage wasn't meant to be. On the one hand, I knew that those thoughts were voices from the enemy, but on the other, I found them very believable because I was experiencing chronic grief.

When it comes to infertility, there are lots of choices and rarely a clear path. Among the questions we dealt with: Do we keep pursuing treatment or wait for a miracle? Do we remain childless and make peace with being a family of two? Do we adopt?

We sought marriage counseling during infertility because neither Mark nor I could see our situation objectively. One of our biggest issues was in communication style, which had been an issue even before infertility but became much bigger when we faced years of childlessness. In fact, the elephant in the room—the issue of infertility—magnified all of the smaller issues we had been able to deal with pretty easily before this challenge.

Our emotional healing took place over time. Ultimately, we resolved our conflicting views about what lengths to go to in order to have children, and we adopted two daughters domestically. In the end, God also blessed us when a friend offered to be a gestational surrogate and carry our biological son. Once we started on the adoption path, our family grew quickly, and we were eventually able to find some peace and heal our relationship.

Sarah's Sweet Surprises

During the long, grueling sadness of her struggle with infertility, treatments, and the long waits between major decisions, Sarah took time to recognize the unanticipated blessings that came her way:

- "Mark never failed to bring me flowers a couple of times a month—his way of adding beauty during the ugliness of infertility."
- "After my tubal pregnancy, I passed out in church and a couple of friends provided meals and came to our home to sit with me until I recovered. That meant more than I can put into words."
- "My mom, who refused to let infertility beat me, threw a huge thirtieth birthday party for me at their home just a couple of days after I was discharged

> from the hospital after my tubal pregnancy. It was in the summertime, and her birthday invitations explicitly said, 'Adults Only.' She wanted me to be able to enjoy the party without thinking about infertility. We sang karaoke on the deck, ate delicious food, and danced until the wee hours. Even though I had just suffered the loss of my twins, the party and all of my friends and family around me allowed me to celebrate my thirty years of life and even to realize that life is worth celebrating, with or without a baby. What a gift!"

Surprised by Joy

God wants to surprise us on a continual basis, loving us and blessing our marriages. Earlier in this chapter we discussed the unexpected negative surprises that can attack a marriage—but we need to remember the other meanings of the word *surprise*. It can mean to astonish, to amaze, to astound, or to strike with wonder by something unlooked for.

As much as we want to plan and control our lives and live out the image of an ideal marriage, God wants to astound us with what he can do through our broken places. As his light shines through the cracks of our imperfect stories, he says, "I can make your relationship better than it ever was before your crisis. I'm going to use you to help other couples experiencing similar circumstances. Your humility and lack of perfection are beautiful to me. Give me all of your unanswered questions, your frustration, your exhaustion, and your pain. I have a plan—and that plan includes great joy!"

Discussion Questions
for Couples and Small Groups

1. What one concept in this chapter most challenged your thinking?
2. Read the inventory questions on page 177. Pick the one you most identify with. Why did you choose that one?
3. We're reminded in this chapter that if we keep God in first place, if we walk in his ways, "all these blessings will . . . overtake [us]" (Deut. 28:2 NASB). The word *overtake* in the original Hebrew carries a sense of *caught by surprise.* In what specific ways has God surprised you in the midst of your journey?
4. In this chapter, Gene and Carol described their two decades of heartache upon heartache, loss upon loss, and dashed hopes. They also explained how they focused on the ways in which God continues to surprise us with blessings—just as all of us need to if we're to survive our crises. Share a story in which God used someone else to surprise you with a delightful and needed blessing.

CHAPTER 9

Say Yes to Guilt-Free Time-Outs

> When we take care of ourselves, we are filled up, renewed, and restored to give to others.
>
> —Olivia Spears

The alarm rang at 5:00 a.m. My body didn't want to do what my mind said it must do—get up! It was a Saturday morning, and Gene and I (Carol) were headed to the prison to stand in that two-hour-long line. If we didn't get there early enough, we wouldn't get through security in time to have the corrections officers call our son to the visitation room before "count time." The inmates are counted multiple times a day, and no prisoners are allowed to move from building to building until the inmate count is accurate. Visitors often have to wait an extra hour and a half to see their loved one if they arrive midmorning.

After nineteen years of visiting our son behind the razor wire of a maximum-security prison, I was tired of this routine. It had been a busy fall, and the past week had been particularly intense. I was physically exhausted and mentally spent. I wanted to see my son, but I felt overwhelmed with the endlessness of his "life without the possibility of parole" sentence.

At times Gene and I felt conflicted. Jason needed our visits; he longed to spend time with us. We love him dearly, but in nineteen years we had never really decided how often we needed to visit. Questions loomed:

- Did we demonstrate a lack of caring if we were home on a Saturday or Sunday (prison visitation days in Florida) without driving the three-hour-and-twenty-minute round-trip to spend several hours with him? On visitation days we left the house at 7:00 a.m. and returned home at 4:30 p.m.
- Was it okay to have family or friends go for visits on weekends without our being at the prison on every visitation day?
- Would our son feel we were disloyal if we visited him less often?

Every couple dealing with an incarcerated child or with a son or daughter with a severe disability has huge decisions to make, and sometimes conflict seems inevitable. We love our kids, but there are times when we reach a complete end of our physical resources. The guilt can be overwhelming. Usually it's self-imposed guilt—but it's still a very heavy mantle.

I chuckled when I looked up the word. "Guilt is a cognitive or an emotional experience that occurs when a person believes or realizes—accurately or not—that they have compromised their own standards of conduct or have violated universal moral standards and bear significant responsibility for that violation."[1] Yup! That's exactly what I was feeling—like *I* was a criminal for not living up to the standard of what a good Christian mother should do to keep her precious son encouraged on his lifetime journey of living behind bars.

I felt tension mounting between Gene and me. "Carol," he said, "our son is an adult who fully realizes that we lead busy lives and have intense demands. He understands that we sometimes need a break after our long workweeks and can't always be physically present at visitation. You're trying to hold yourself to an impossible standard."

I knew he was right, but I resisted. "I want him to know how much he's loved and that we thoroughly enjoy spending time with him."

Gene's advice was good. He reminded me that we talk to our son by phone four or five times a week. "I think our relationship with Jason is extremely close," he said, "because when we're together, sitting at a table in the visitation room, we talk for hours about family, personal, and spiritual matters—and we've formed a bond that many families have never had time to develop. Don't you think Jason would rather have you *all there* when you visit, rather than exhausted?"

I knew he was right—but it was still hard to figure out the right balance, to find the visitation schedule that met our son's needs and still allowed us time to breathe.

Then Gene spoke the truth that brought real clarity: "Carol, for the rest of our lives or until Jason's sentence ends, we're in this together. There will be weekends when I can visit him by myself, or other times when you need some private mom/son time and I'll stay home. And there are going to be visitation weekends when we need to step back and rest due to the extreme demands of life and ministry. And when that happens, we have to guard against being legalistic about what constitutes good parenting.

"When we take care of ourselves, we'll be able to visit Jason feeling like we have energy and encouragement to give because we're rested. And when that happens, all three of us will benefit from seeing each other. You're a firstborn. You're a driven woman, and that's part of what first attracted me to you. I don't know anybody who gets more done than you, and you've accomplished a lot in your lifetime. But firstborn or not, if you don't take the time to get filled up yourself, sometimes you'll have nothing to offer to Jason or to others. I know Jason wants to see you when you're rested and relaxed, not when you're falling asleep at a table in the visitation room."

Was Gene right? I knew immediately that he was. But finding the balance is still hard.

Conflicted Thinking

Susan, a wife and mom from Fort Wayne, Indiana, is in her early fifties. She says:

> I grew up in a home where I never heard the term "self-care." I knew that my parents, who were in ministry, were passionate about reaching people in our community with the gospel message. I often heard sermons on "giving ourselves away" for

kingdom purposes. The idea of being intentional about taking time for rest, relaxation, and quiet time as a married couple had no place in my value system. In fact, I believed making time for mental breaks and physical "breathers" was selfish.

My husband, on the other hand, looks at life very differently—and that difference creates conflict—lots of it.

Two and a half years ago, my eighty-one-year-old widowed mother moved in with us. She's been diagnosed with Alzheimer's and needs a lot of supervision and companionship. Combine that with the needs of our three school-aged children, and at times I feel unable to cope with all of the personal and ministry pressures in my life.

When Joe has completed a long day's work, he has no problem with kicking off his shoes, letting voicemail take messages for after-hours calls, and watching a movie on Netflix. He gets agitated when I don't join him because I'm dealing with my mother's needs or trying to catch up on what has to be done around the house or preparing for a church activity. He says, "Even Jesus didn't heal everybody in the crowd who had a physical need. He took breaks and spent time with his Father and with his disciples."

A Checklist

As a couple, go through these statements and decide which ones apply to you—individually, and/or as a couple. Remember that you may disagree (imagine!) about whether the statement applies to you. Determine ahead of time not to allow this discussion to become an argument.

- When I relax, I feel guilty.[2]
- It's okay to not be okay—and to admit it to each other and to others.

- Even when I'm doing nothing, I'm always doing something.
- Even when I reach the point that my brain is fried, I'm still able to relax.
- I have trouble enjoying my sexual relationship with my spouse when our current family crisis isn't resolved yet.
- When my services are in high demand by family, friends, or coworkers, I have a hard time saying no to their requests, even when I'm exhausted.
- It's difficult for me to take a movie break when I'm stressed over what's going on in our lives.
- It feels wrong to go on a vacation or to enjoy a getaway weekend when our challenging situation isn't resolved.
- We don't seem to face crises with the same intensity. I get irritated when my spouse seems (to me at least) obsessed with our circumstances. Life will always have its difficulties, but we need to relax, laugh out loud, and have fun once in a while.

Drawing Together during Tough Times

Tough times trigger unanticipated emotions: tempers flare, the blame-game starts, anxiety is heightened—or the silent treatment keeps us locked up and unreachable. When our son was arrested, we (Carol and Gene) experienced false shame, thinking there must have been something we could have done through better parenting that would have kept him from making such a horrible choice. What is *false shame*? In our case it was feeling like spiritual failures over a decision our son made—a decision we wished we could have prevented before it resulted in devastating consequences. As parents, it's easy to experience irrational feelings of inadequacy and self-doubt, even when it's not us but our children who make unwise and/or destructive choices.

When our friends James and Heather found themselves dealing with the growing tensions of raising a severely autistic daughter, they often blew up at each other, turning nonissues into issues and allowing minor irritations to become impossible obstacles. The day they walked into their family room and discovered that Sophie had smeared her bowel movement on the wall, they started yelling angrily, blaming each other for not maintaining order and civility in their home.

Here are a few suggestions that we hope will *reduce* the pressure you feel rather than increase it.

Develop a daily habit that takes you away from the immediate stress of your ongoing situation.

An important part of our growth as a couple in the initial stages of our challenge was to go on walks together, praying out loud as we walked side by side. One of us would pray, "God, we are afraid for our son. We fear for his safety. We don't know where the money for his trial will come from." The other would then pray, "Lord, you are good and you are trustworthy. We know nothing can touch us without your permission, but our hearts agonize—for the family of the deceased and for our son. Right now we ask, *Why? Why did you allow this to happen?*" Making a habit of praying together and asking God our honest questions made our marriage stronger. It was a time-out with God.

Accept help from others.

James and Heather, our friends raising an autistic daughter, discovered that they couldn't allow their challenges with Sophie to place a wedge between them. They have three other children who desire and need their love and care too. They also needed time with each other *apart* from the ongoing challenges of raising a child with a severe disability. At first, trying to manage everything themselves, they lived in a constant state of exhaustion. Heather said, "Then I researched all of the educational and social options for Sophie that would fit our budget—and she's now in school and in other programs part of every day. She's happier and we're calmer."

James and Heather also started accepting the help of a sister (Sophie's aunt) who volunteered to come to their home to provide child care one night a week so they could go out for dinner or see a movie without worrying about the kids. They came home refreshed and were better able to face the day-to-day stress.

Communicate with other couples who understand your challenges.

Gene says: One of the most helpful things Carol and I experienced was getting to know other married couples who had an incarcerated child. After all, we spent a lot of time standing in the prison visitation line, waiting to get through the security point, and in those hours we met lots of couples going through the same ordeal. The frustration of standing in that long line became a bonding experience as we shared our stories with each other. We shared our irritation with an inefficient prison system, the financial challenges of going through the trial, and the expense of keeping enough money in an inmate's account for basic needs. We asked the couples we met what they did to deal with their stress.

Their responses were painfully honest. One woman said, "I cope with my sadness by drinking too much." Another said, "I just try not to think about it or I'd be a basket case every day." On days when we all shared honestly about how difficult our journey is, we experienced a time-out—*away* from anyone who might judge us for being bad parents, and *with* people who could vent about their situation, knowing that talking to us was a safe place to speak out loud about their difficulties.

What Did Jesus Say and Do?

For those of us whose approach to life, marriage, and the tough spots of life is grounded in faith, there's an example we can look to that provides a noteworthy illustration of how to take guilt-free time-outs in the middle of conflict, stress, dealing with demanding people, and the harsh realities of our true-life situations. If we really believe that we are meant to live as Jesus lived, we need to study how he made time to get away from the demands of people in search of solitude and how he valued time with his Father.

- *Jesus made time alone with God a high priority.*

  Before daybreak the next morning, Jesus got up and went out to an isolated place to pray. (Mark 1:35 NLT)

> The apostles returned to Jesus from their ministry tour and told him all they had done and taught. Then Jesus said, "Let's go off by ourselves to a quiet place and rest awhile." He said this because there were so many people coming and going that Jesus and his apostles didn't even have time to eat. So they left by boat for a quiet place, where they could be alone. (Mark 6:30–32 NLT)

- *Jesus slept in the middle of stormy, chaotic surroundings.*

  > Then Jesus got into the boat and started across the lake with his disciples. Suddenly, a fierce storm struck the lake, with waves breaking into the boat. But Jesus was sleeping. The disciples went and woke him up, shouting, "Lord, save us! We're going to drown!"
  >
  > Jesus responded, "Why are you afraid? You have so little faith!" Then he got up and rebuked the wind and waves, and suddenly there was a great calm. (Matt. 8:23–26 NLT)

- *Jesus promised rest for all who are willing to come to him.*

  > Then Jesus said, "Come to me, all of you who are weary and carry heavy burdens, and I will give you rest." (Matt. 11:28 NLT)

- *Jesus fed the disciples while they were in the middle of wrapping their heads around the mystery of his death and resurrection.*

  > He called out, "Fellows, have you caught any fish?"

> "No," they replied.
>
> Then he said, "Throw out your net on the right-hand side of the boat, and you'll get some!" So they did, and they couldn't haul in the net because there were so many fish in it.
>
> Then the disciple Jesus loved said to Peter, "It's the Lord!" When Simon Peter heard that it was the Lord, he put on his tunic (for he had stripped for work), jumped into the water, and headed to shore. The others stayed with the boat and pulled the loaded net to the shore, for they were only about a hundred yards from shore. When they got there, they found breakfast waiting for them—fish cooking over a charcoal fire, and some bread.
>
> "Bring some of the fish you've just caught," Jesus said. So Simon Peter went aboard and dragged the net to the shore. There were 153 large fish, and yet the net hadn't torn.
>
> "Now come and have some breakfast!" Jesus said. None of the disciples dared to ask him, "Who are you?" They knew it was the Lord. Then Jesus served them the bread and the fish. This was the third time Jesus had appeared to his disciples since he had been raised from the dead. (John 21:5–14 NLT)

Friends, I think that in those passages and others like them Jesus gave us all the instruction and example about rest we need as married couples dealing with any kind of interruption, crisis, challenge, or hard circumstances. A few things jumped off the page for me (Carol) in those passages. First, it's okay with God if we take time to sleep, to eat, and to pull away from our chaotic situations. He modeled how to do just that! And second, even though he was extremely busy and people often clamored for his attention, he made the time for restorative activities that brought rejuvenation and fresh focus to him and to his disciples in the middle of stressful circumstances.

He even goes a step further. He says: "Come to me, all of you who are weary and carry heavy burdens" (Matt. 11:28 NLT). In order to live successfully in the middle of all of the challenges we face, our greatest necessity is to have a time-out with God. Bring him your exhaustion and voice your need for wisdom, clarity, and direction. He longs to hear your voice. He cares, even when life isn't making any sense.

Figuring Out How to Survive

You may be thinking, *Our lives are so consumed with dealing with our challenges, there's no way we could ever take a guilt-free time-out*. Sometimes it helps to start out by using a marriage assessment tool. Find out what you're doing well, where you need improvement, where you're satisfied, and what's making you feel unfulfilled. Focus on the Family offers an excellent survey at https://assessments.focusonthefamily.com/s3/focus-on-marriage-assessment.

For Gene and me, the details and pressures of our son's incarceration felt like a treadmill we couldn't get off. We felt as if we were getting nothing done. Busyness became an important part of our survival—but not in the best way. We *deliberately avoided* downtime. If we didn't fill our days with a long to-do list and mandatory assignments dealing with our crisis, we would have to stop long enough to think about what our future might look like. And *that* was painful. A destructive cycle of frightening thoughts would overwhelm us.

- *If we were better parents, could we have stopped our son's crime from happening?*
- *Should we be open and honest about our journey or keep our story a secret?*
- *How will our finances be affected by this?*
- *What possible hope for a happy life will our son ever have?*
- *Will our marriage ever be stress-free, or will we live in a constant state of turmoil for the rest of our lives?*

Those swirling questions made us focus more on the problem and not on finding the ways for our marriage to not only survive but *thrive* despite horrible circumstances that could not be changed.

One day we took a walk and talked openly about our lives and our marriage. Some things were abundantly clear to us both. For one, we needed to stop living constantly in crisis mode. Also, we urgently needed to take time to focus on each other. And another thing we agreed on wholeheartedly is that we wanted to laugh again; we wanted humor to become as big a part of our lives as it had been earlier in our marriage. Gene, a lover of adventure, wanted us to be purposeful about planning some getaways. I confess that I shrugged that off, saying, "Sometimes it just feels wrong to enjoy ourselves with our son behind bars—especially if it's something we deliberately plan." We didn't find answers to all of our questions that day, but we knew that we'd taken a big step. Our conversation had been healthy, and the ways we could build a future together were a little more clear.

Besides—it *felt good.* We were talking out loud about our fears, our failures, our lost dreams, and our questions. We'd been focused for so long on our son and what we could do for him in this horrible situation, but now it was time to make intentional plans focused on ourselves and our need for a fulfilling, happy marriage, even though no magic wand would change the reality of our son's incarceration. Moving forward would require both of us to understand that our new normal would not be what we'd envisioned when we said our marriage vows. But that didn't mean we were sentenced to an unhappy life.

We walked back to the house and paused in the kitchen. Gene put his arms around my waist and kissed the back of my neck. Holding me tenderly, he began to pray: "Lord, you have blessed my life with Carol, and she's precious to me. Help us to not lose the joy we have in each other as we deal with the pressures of Jason's long prison sentence. Teach me to be attentive to her needs. Help us to be responsive to each other. Father, will you bring daily doses of laughter back into our lives? Give us creativity as we plan for breaks that are restorative and healing. When we focus on each other and our future together, save us from false guilt. Help us to realize how much we're pleasing you when we give attention to building our marriage. We love you and want to honor you with our lives. Amen."

A surprising peace swept over me, and I sighed. Gene and I were on the same page; we were going to focus on each other in meaningful ways. It wouldn't be easy to change the obsessive way we had been trying to manage all of the details of our son's incarceration, but we were committed to taking positive steps to focus on each other. We both wanted a happy marriage, and we would do what was necessary to foster positive change in the ways we'd been responding to each other.

Joe and Kim's Story

We are the parents of four adopted children—two boys and two girls. We learned that Anna was intellectually challenged at age five, and she was diagnosed with schizophrenia at age seven. Sadly, her abilities have deteriorated over the years.

For a while, medications helped her to stabilize. Our search for the perfect mix of medications continues—we've struggled to find a med that is totally effective in controlling her hallucinations.

Looking back, we've had quite a journey navigating her needs and the changing seasons in her life. Our marriage is like a lens, one of many we can choose to look through to see how God has worked in us as individuals and as a couple. It has been for many years a roller coaster of emotions and experiences, and over that time my [Kim's] biggest comfort has been having an ally in my husband, Joe—an ally who shares the exact same vantage point.

Together, we've experienced all of the joys and challenges of raising our daughter. We love meeting with other special-needs parents. Even though each family has different experiences and different needs, we learn from each other and identify with the uniqueness of our challenges. We relate to each other in deep ways, and I always find that encouraging.

My husband and I are the gatekeepers of all that pertains to our daughter. We realized many years ago we could do it alone, or we could do it together. We could do it leaning on each other, trusting each other, finding joy in the camaraderie of it all, or we could become emotional loners. We certainly have small disagreements about decisions we need to make concerning our daughter, but we are confident that we can agree and move forward together.

Together is better, for her and for us. We have cried together in our private moments, but more often we laugh together—or smile as we give each other knowing glances that it's time to take our daughter out of a restaurant or a church service. We often don't need words anymore; we have found an intimacy I would have never known with my husband apart from our daughter.

So if we are picking teams, I pick Joe. He's my accomplice, partner, companion, and parent-in-crime. We usually agree on such things as when it's time to take the easy road and quiet our daughter with a donut or soda pop. It may have been the deep, hard things with our daughter that built our foundation, but the daily little things have strengthened it. And if you want to challenge us over the donut and soda pop, we can always use a date night and our daughter would be happy to meet someone new. I promise—you will be looking for the nearest donut shop!

A Run-In with Guilt

Joe and Kim's story continues:

I'd love to tell you I've never had to deal with guilt, but that would be a lie. It somehow feels wrong to take care of ourselves instead of keeping our focus on our daughter.

For example: We were planning a family trip and, because of Anna's special needs, we were considering leaving her at home with her grandma. Our other three children were coming with us; Anna would be the only one not coming. And in truth, Anna doesn't like to travel. Still, to take a family trip without her seemed wrong.

As the date of the trip came closer, I was on an emotional roller coaster, and I kept putting off the final decision. But in the end, Joe and I decided: we would go, and we would leave Anna with her grandma. I felt horribly guilty. At first, I wasn't willing to call it a "family" vacation. Thoughts crept in: *It's wrong to have fun without her. If I worry the whole time, I will feel like a better mom. What if Grandma can't use the TV remote control properly to find Anna's favorite shows?*

A day into the trip, I couldn't believe how enjoyable it was. By the second day, I whispered my confession to Joe: "I'm having fun! It's so nice to sit in a restaurant and not have to cut up Anna's food or worry that she's getting agitated."

By the end of the trip, I was having moments of pure bliss and didn't care who knew. Now, months later, I'm willing to declare it out loud: I had an amazing trip and enjoyed every single minute of it. It was good for our marriage and it allowed us, as a couple, to give our other children the undivided attention they need. We had time with them in a fresh, wonderful way. I had not considered that they might need a break from the constant pressure of being "the helpful siblings," the ones who frequently had to leave restaurants before they'd finished their meals due to their sister's inappropriate behavior. They needed to know it wasn't necessary for them to skip fun adventures because those things might not be appropriate for their sister.

One of the best results of the trip was that Grandma treated Anna like a princess, and I don't think we were even missed. It took me a long time to fully understand how much this trip brought me the break I needed in the middle of long-term caregiving. After this experience, I'm letting go of guilt—and Grandma is already booked for next year.

Kim's Confession

Before wrapping up her story, Kim mentioned that she and Joe still struggle with one issue—and isn't that just what guilt does? Just when we think we've called guilt out and put it in its box, one small thought lingers in the back of our minds like a tiny stone in our shoe, causing false shame.

For Kim and Joe, that issue involved family pictures. They didn't want to take any family photos without having Anna included. It somehow felt like intentionally leaving out an important member of the family. Kim explained:

> Why do I mention this after all of the positives we've experienced? Because it reminds Joe and me that we still have room to grow as a couple and as a family, and that we need to regularly ask God for his help. So next year we're determined to take more group photos of our family—and we're going to help Grandma develop her selfie skills so we can exchange more photos with Anna when we're away. We're going to embrace change and choose joy over guilt.

Creating Guilt-Free Time-Outs

After the first shock of Jason's incarceration and as Gene and I began to seek the ways to adjust to our new normal, we realized that we had to build our marriage in small ways. When we looked at the big picture—that our son was sentenced to be in prison for the rest of his life—we knew we faced a lifetime challenge ourselves. Would we learn to take time-outs and nurture our marriage while still meeting Jason's needs, or would we allow exhaustion and anxiety to erode our once-solid marriage? We discovered it was best to start in small ways, including the ways I've listed below. We hope they will be helpful to you too.

- *Seek God first.* Choose a devotional for you and your spouse.[3] Select a time in the day when both of you commit to sharing the daily reading and suggested Scripture together. Take turns praying aloud and be specific about mentioning each other's needs. This won't take a lot of time, and it will make every other part of your day better.
- *Take short breaks outside and breathe deeply.* Say to yourself, "Some things will not get done today, and that's okay."
- *Go out for coffee with your spouse* and list everything you have to be thankful for. We were amazed at how often people assisted us in small ways and helped to carry our load. That reaffirmed our understanding of the support we had and brought a surge of hope.
- *Take turns.* When your tough situation creates major stress, take turns coping. Ask, "How are you doing?" We usually know when our partner is at the ragged edge of his or her last nerve. When one of you needs a break, let the other handle the tough stuff for an hour or for a day.

- *Plan a getaway together.* It doesn't have to be a long trip. It could be a few hours at a park or an overnight away from your daily responsibilities.
- *Delegate some tasks.* Sometimes we think we're the only people who can handle the details connected to our challenges, whether it be aging parents, health issues for those we love, incarceration of a loved one, or special-needs children. That's not true. Research what programs are available and who could assist—not just paid professionals, but volunteers who want to help.
- *Find a conference or retreat you can attend as a couple* that will nourish your hearts spiritually. Sign up and then work on the arrangements that will free you to go. A great choice is to attend a Weekend to Remember, sponsored by Family Life Ministries. You'll find a date and location that may work for you here: https://www.familylife.com/weekend-to-remember.
- *Take mini time-outs.* Ask yourself: *What brings me joy?* For Gene, it's reading a chapter of a great book. For Carol, it's playing *Words with Friends* and sharpening her vocabulary. When we take even fifteen to thirty minutes away from our ongoing stressor, we are better able to cope with daily life.
- *Remove three items from your to-do list today.* The tasks will eventually get done—but with the extra time this gives you today, call an "energy-giving" friend and catch up on each other's lives. Or take a guilt-free nap. Or do a crossword puzzle. Or take a walk or a bike ride. Later, share the experience with your spouse.

A Final Thought

Taking care of ourselves—mentally, physically, emotionally, and spiritually—puts us on track to fulfill the command to "'love the LORD your God with all your heart, all your soul, all your strength, and all your mind.' And, 'Love your neighbor as yourself'" (Luke 10:27 NLT). We start to recognize how much God values us and to understand that when we take care of ourselves, individually and as a married couple, we are better equipped to love our family members and everyone around us in a healthy way.

Discussion Questions *for* Couples and Small Groups

1. What action step will you take as a result of reading this chapter?
2. How different (or similar) are you from your spouse in your ability to take guilt-free time-outs?
3. Discuss how much of your typical day or week is characterized by anxiety, fatigue, overwork, stress, and worry. Now read and discuss Mark 6:30–31 NLT: "The apostles returned to Jesus from their ministry tour and told him all they had done and taught. Then Jesus said, 'Let's go off by ourselves to a quiet place and rest awhile.' He said this because there were so many people coming and going that Jesus and his apostles didn't even have time to eat." Talk through how your typical schedule as individuals and

as couples might be made to resemble more closely Jesus's words: "Let's go off by ourselves to a quiet place and rest awhile."

4. Review the checklist on pages 187–88 and select one that you would like to work on. Why did you choose that one?

CHAPTER 10

Never Give Up

> When you get into a tight place and everything goes against you, till it seems as though you could not hang on a minute longer, never give up then, for that is just the place and time that the tide will turn.
>
> —Harriet Beecher Stowe

Stan and Rachel's marriage had never been easy. But when her biological son—Stan's stepson—Isaac was arrested and charged with sexual assault, on a date, of a female student a couple of years younger, all hell broke loose. Stan talked at length with Isaac, with the girl's parents, with the arresting officer and prosecuting attorney, and even with the attorney they'd hired to represent Isaac. Those conversations convinced him that things had happened pretty much as the girl had said. Isaac had sullenly all but admitted it.

But for Rachel, that was all irrelevant. This was her *son*! And whatever he was accused of, the only position she was willing to accept was complete commitment to defending him against all accusations, even if he wasn't defending himself.

"Of course he's not defending himself!" she shouted. "He's scared to death!"

"I'm sure he is," Stan said, "but he told me he—"

"What's wrong with you! He's terrified! He doesn't know what he's saying! When he can't stand up for himself, it's your job to do it for him! Don't you realize that if he's convicted of this, you can kiss his academic scholarship for next year goodbye?"

In the end, the girl's family was reluctant to have her testify, and Isaac's attorney agreed to probation.

Over the next few months Stan watched as Rachel pulled gradually further and further away. Eventually, she had no interest in spending time with him at all, and her emotional attitude toward him had gone beyond *indifferent* all the way to *cold*. He had tried talking to her about it, had asked her pointedly and directly what was wrong, but she always either gave no response whatsoever or shrugged and declined to discuss it. The state of their marriage was dire, and if Stan wanted to save it, for not just his sake but the whole family's, something had to be done.

He suggested counseling.

Rachel shook her head. "I've suggested that a couple of times in past years, and you didn't have any interest in it then."

"I know. I'm sorry. I was wrong. We should have done it then, but we should definitely do it now."

She studied him for a moment. *The first eye contact we've had in weeks,* he thought. Then she said, "I don't see the point. It won't change anything."

"We won't know until we try," he said.

She sighed and stood up. "No," she said. "You're never going to change. Talking about it is pointless." She started to walk away.

"I don't understand. You talk like you've given up on our marriage," Stan said.

Rachel turned around. "If you mean do I want a divorce—no. That wouldn't be fair to the kids. They've suffered enough. But have I given up on the idea that we'll ever have a workable, rewarding marriage? Absolutely." She started away again, then turned and looked back at him. "If only you had at least *pretended* to take his side, to believe in him. For his sake." She left the room.

Stan *was* willing to change, or at least to take a run at it. He had concerns about Rachel's behavior and attitudes, too, and frankly he didn't expect her to change either, but he could live with that. He knew this much—he wasn't going to give up on their marriage.

And that's when he realized that *never giving up* was even more complicated than that—more complicated than he'd ever realized. He was determined to never give up on their marriage. But had he already all but given up on the stepson whose misbehavior had provoked what his wife clearly saw as the "last straw" in a shaky marriage? How many times since the resolution of the case against Isaac had Stan sat down with him to check in, seriously, on how he was doing, how the bad choices he had made were affecting his emotions, his relationships? Almost none. Was Isaac doing the same thing now with a different young woman? Was he tempted? Was he channeling his sex drive in positive directions, or negative? Was he depressed, angry, discouraged? In fact, once the court case was resolved, Stan had figured he'd devoted as much time to that situation as he could afford and turned his attention and energy toward their other kids and his and Rachel's parents and bills and the house and his job and . . .

And he'd basically given up on his stepson's struggles. But his wife had not. She still rejected the idea that Isaac had been guilty and fully believed that he was the victim of a scheming, immoral young woman and a witch hunt by a lazy police department. But despite what Stan saw as her willful self-delusion about her son's behavior and guilt, she was faithful about spending time with him, propping him up, being his cheerleader and "mama bear" protector. Stan had given up—but his wife had not. What had his lack of involvement communicated to his wife? How might things have been different now, Stan wondered, if he had thrown himself into his stepson's rehabilitation with determination and commitment and, yes, true affection, no matter what it took and regardless of whether he thought Isaac had been guilty? *But we have other kids who were ignored for months while we sorted things out for Isaac with the courts,* he thought. And then he found himself remembering the parable of the lost sheep:

> Suppose one of you has a hundred sheep and loses one of them. Doesn't he leave the ninety-nine in the open country and go after the lost sheep until he finds it? And when he finds it, he joyfully puts it on his shoulders and goes home. Then he calls his friends and neighbors together and says, "Rejoice with me; I have found my lost sheep." I tell you that in the same way there will be more rejoicing in heaven

> over one sinner who repents than over ninety-nine righteous persons who do not need to repent. (Luke 15:4–7)

Never Give Up. Never Give In.

Most of us have heard the story of Winston Churchill's famous "Never give up" speech, and we've probably all heard different versions of it. Odd, considering that there are recordings of it, so in fact we know exactly what he said and didn't say. I (Dave) remember hearing once that the entire speech, start to finish, consisted of: "Never give up. Never give up. Never, never, never, never." And then he sat down. Not quite accurate. Churchill did say that, or something close to it, but the speech he gave at Harrow School on October 29, 1941, actually lasted for twenty minutes. Part of his speech ran:

> Never give in. Never give in. Never, never, never, never—in nothing great or small, large or petty—never give in, except to convictions of honour and good sense. Never yield to force. Never yield to the apparently overwhelming might of the enemy.[1]

And that quotation reminds me of another. Both are essential to understanding what attitude we must take to overcome the challenges life throws at our marriages. This one comes from M. Scott Peck in his bestselling book *The Road Less Traveled*:

> Life is difficult. This is a great truth, one of the greatest truths. It is a great truth because once we truly see this truth, we

> transcend it. Once we truly know that life is difficult—once we truly understand and accept it—then life is no longer difficult. Because once it is accepted, the fact that life is difficult no longer matters.[2]

From those two remarkable quotations, we can extract two principles that are essential if as married couples we are to maneuver through life effectively:

1. It is certain that we will face hard things in life and in marriage—things that will test us and that will threaten to overpower us.
2. We can't let the challenges of life win. No matter how hard the fight, no matter how overwhelming the odds, we must never give up.

The words *never give up* can be applied to the trials of life and their effects on our marriage in two ways.

First, *never give up* on your marriage. You encounter in the stories in this book couples who clung to each other and to their marriage with stubborn insistence and unfailing hope that things would get better. And you encounter others who, like Rachel in the story that began this chapter, have given up on their marriage. Our first chapter stated a bedrock principle of this book: we're in this together. Never give up on your spouse. Never give up on your marriage.

And second, *never give up* on defending your marriage and your family against the challenges life throws at you, no matter how difficult they are—and some of them are giants. Winston Churchill was speaking about a different kind of war, but his words are as applicable to the war in defense of your marriage: *Never yield to the apparently overwhelming might of the enemy.*

Perseverance

When the Bible speaks of never giving up, it sometimes calls that *perseverance*. Here's an activity that might help you and your spouse cement that idea into your minds. We've listed below a number of Bible verses that speak of this key character trait. Read through them together and discuss what these verses mean and how they apply to your marriage. Are there specific things you've faced—or are facing—that these verses put into perspective?

> So do not fear, for I am with you;
>   do not be dismayed, for I am your God.
> I will strengthen you and help you;
>   I will uphold you with my righteous right hand.
>   (Isa. 41:10)

> Truly I tell you, if you have faith as small as a mustard seed, you can say to this mountain, "Move from here to there," and it will move. Nothing will be impossible for you. (Matt. 17:20)

> Let us not become weary in doing good, for at the proper time we will reap a harvest if we do not give up. (Gal. 6:9)

> Whatever happens, conduct yourselves in a manner worthy of the gospel of Christ. Then, whether I come and see you or only hear about you in my absence, I will know that you stand firm in the one Spirit, striving together as one for the

> faith of the gospel without being frightened in any way by those who oppose you. (Phil. 1:27–28)

> For the Spirit God gave us does not make us timid, but gives us power, love and self-discipline. (2 Tim. 1:7)

> Let us hold unswervingly to the hope we profess, for he who promised is faithful. And let us consider how we may spur one another on toward love and good deeds. . . . So do not throw away your confidence; it will be richly rewarded. You need to persevere so that when you have done the will of God, you will receive what he has promised. (Heb. 10:23–24, 35–36)

Where the Rubber Meets the Road

Stan and Rachel didn't save their marriage. I say *didn't* rather than *couldn't,* because I believe that almost every marriage can be saved if both parties are willing to try. Stan even went so far as to make an appointment with a marriage counselor just to ask whether counseling would do any good if only *he* came, since Rachel wouldn't come with him. The counselor's predictable response: "Marriage counseling only works if both parties participate."

But that doesn't mean there was nothing Stan could do if his wife wasn't yet at a point where she could support the idea of reconciliation. He could pray. He could reach out to her in a variety of ways that wouldn't require enthusiasm or participation on her part—such as cooking her favorite meal, or giving her some small, thoughtful gift. He could try hard to intuit what things about their family, about Stan himself, were sticking in her craw, and then come up with a game plan to openly address those things differently—not simply as a way to bring her back, because that would just reinforce what she was probably already thinking about him ("He's not sincere—whenever you think he's doing the right thing, look for the ulterior motive"), but as a genuine effort to address the issues facing their family and thereby make things better for them all.

Stan had to admit that although he was strong in his commitment to their marriage, he was sometimes weak in recognizing and withstanding the threats against that marriage. His marriage definitely needed both. But Stan was so singularly focused on the problems between Rachel and himself that he ignored or dismissed or simply forgot about the other threats facing them. In other words, he gave up on those issues. Stan—and all of us—could improve our ability to be our family's first line of defense by improving our resistance to the all-too-easy response to tough challenges: giving up. Here are some suggestions:

Keep your eyes on the prize.

Sports fans, when you're watching one of your favorite teams compete for a championship, and your team's players seem to be competing at low energy, watching their chance at stardom slip away, don't you feel like pulling your hair out? What's the matter with them? Can't they imagine the parades, the interviews, the magazine covers, the applause and cheering they'll receive if they fight it out to the last moment, leave everything on the field, every last ounce of effort—and win, preferably on the last play of the game? If they just refuse to *give up*? And even if they lose—they'll know they did everything they could.

If you feel like giving up on whatever conflict is threatening your marriage or your family, it may be because, like that team, you've taken your eyes off the goal. You have a spouse and, perhaps, children who are depending on you to put in the effort, take the steps, and make the adjustments necessary to protect your family from whatever threatens it. *Never give up*. Keep playing at 100 percent effort till the clock expires.

And if you've forgotten what the prize is, ask yourself: *Why am I doing this? Why is it worth it? Who else is depending on me? What will I lose if I just give up now? What do I gain if I stick with it till I've accomplished my goal?*

What doesn't kill you makes you stronger.

Okay, we've all heard that said so many times it has almost lost its meaning. And that's a shame, because it's a powerful meaning. Think of life, for a moment, as a trip to the gym. Pumping those weights, putting in the effort on the stair-stepper or treadmill or elliptical trainer, you might feel tapped out and think about quitting early. But you don't, because you have a goal in mind—weight loss, or better fitness, or a more sculpted body. The effort you're putting in now will help get you there. You urge yourself on: *Only three more minutes and then I've finished. Don't quit now! Only three minutes! You can do it!*

And the challenges of life and marriage are much the same. Those challenges are "life's gym." They're your workout. And the goals are building a stronger, healthier marriage and family, finding a new normal, and not letting life defeat you. Yes, it's going to take you longer than a one-hour workout. But like any exercise, it has an end point. You'll finish. And when you do, you'll meet your "marriage fitness" goal. Don't give up.

The fact that things are getting tough is no reason to give up.

We all know this cliché: "When the going gets tough, the tough get going." Too often, it could be restated: "When the going gets tough, the would-be tough give up." The truth is, the closer you are to overcoming some major challenge, the tougher things feel. As Marc Chernoff says in "10 Hard Things to Remember When You Feel Like Giving Up," "These intimate, intricate aspects of life are toughest when you're doing them right—when you're dedicating time, having the tough conversations, and making daily sacrifices."[3]

Stay flexible.

If you keep banging your head against a brick wall and accomplishing nothing except giving yourself a monumental headache, then of course you'll eventually want to give up. And maybe you should—at least on the tactics you're using. When approach number one proves to be impossible, don't keep trying it just one more time, and one more time. Keep the goal but discard the tactic and find another way to get past that wall. Maybe there's a tree nearby with a limb that extends over the wall; you could climb the tree, crawl out onto the limb, drop down. Step away from the tactic that isn't working for you and your spouse and regroup. Find approach number two. Plan B.

Give yourselves credit.

If you and your spouse are facing a huge life challenge and ultimate victory is still some way off, don't despair because you haven't yet slain that dragon. Instead, give yourselves credit for all of the steps you've accomplished along the path toward that victory. Each of those small victories has brought you one step closer.

Recognize that some life challenges can never be completely overcome.

Some illnesses, injuries, and losses will be with you for the rest of your life. You can learn new ways of coping with those injuries—but you can't make them go away, and they may limit you. A family member lost to death or incarceration isn't going to magically be restored to you. You will always feel that loss. But that doesn't mean that your family can't find a new normal that allows you to function effectively and even happily as a family. Faced with a permanent challenge such as those, *defeat* is not in the fact that you can't make it go away. *Defeat* would be an inability to rise above it and reclaim your integrity as a couple, as a family, and find again the joy that is your spiritual birthright.

Center Stage in My Own Worst Nightmare

In the fall of 2013, Lisa and Lee Warren lost their son Mitch—Lee's son from a previous marriage. He was nineteen. Lee tells about learning of Mitch's death in his 2020 book *I've Seen the End of You*:

Attending Auburn proved to be too much freedom for him. He made poor choices and ultimately left school and went back to old friends and old habits. For nearly a year, he had little to do with us. Lisa and I texted and called him every day. He rarely answered. . . .

And then, on the morning of August 19, 2013, my phone rang. I looked at the screen and saw MITCH.

"Hey, Mitch!" I said.

"Dad. I want to come home."

Few moments in my lifetime have impacted me as deeply as hearing my son say those words. We talked for an hour, and he told me that he realized how much we'd tried to help him, and that he felt ashamed of himself for not listening, for leaving school, for using drugs. He wanted to go back to Auburn, finish his degree, get his life back on track. He was coming home in three days.

"I love you, Mitch, and I'm so proud of you," I said.

"I'll see you Thursday. I love you, Dad," he said, the last words I ever heard him say. . . .

When the phone rang that evening, when I saw my ex-wife's number on the screen, even when the thought flashed through my mind how unusual it was for her to call me anytime, let alone at night, I never anticipated the news I was about to receive. . . .

I can, as I type these words, hear her sobbing, desperate voice.

"Mitchell is dead."

In that moment, I went from being an observer of other people's troubles, a coach in their hard times, a counselor in their distress, a person who intervenes in life-threatening problems and then goes home at night to his own safe world, to being center stage in my own worst nightmare.[4]

Lisa and Lee continued the story in a recent conversation. Lee said:

> We still don't really know what happened, and that's one of the hardest parts. He was found in a house with another boy with whom he had been friends since kindergarten. Neither had ever been violent with the other. Both had been stabbed, Mitch multiple times, and the other boy once. The drug scans were negative. There was no alcohol involved.
>
> We've never been able to wrap our heads around what happened, and the police really weren't much help.
>
> As soon as it happened, what I wanted was to turn inward and grieve. And the grief was overpowering—I thought it would push me into oblivion. But I didn't have that luxury. We had four other kids. And in fact, our oldest daughter had our first grandchild the day we buried Mitch. So we had a brand-new grandchild we hadn't even met yet because we were in Alabama and Caitlyn was going into labor in San Antonio when Mitch died. We had no idea how to lead our family through this—no sense of confidence that we would make it through it ourselves. But our family still needed us.
>
> It was as if the Lord was saying, "Yes, you have to grieve and process this, but you still have to take care of your family, still have to take care of your spouse, still have to be excited by your new grandchild, love your daughter who has just become a mom for the first time—all those things. And no, it won't be easy. It won't even feel possible. Do it anyway. I'll be there. In fact, I'm already there."
>
> And we just kept moving. We kept doing what we do—go to church, work out in the mornings, be together in the evenings, do stuff with our kids. We tried to maintain some sort of routine. And I think that really helped.

Lisa and Lee had been married seven years when Mitch died. Second marriages for both. They'd had custody of Mitch and his younger sister since about 2008, so he had lived with them, grown up with them, gone to high school while living at their house.

Lee continued:

> Right after Mitch's death, we took maybe three weeks off. But we realized after a couple of weeks that if we didn't get back to work soon our business would be in trouble—I have a solo medical practice as a neurosurgeon, and at the time, while we were living in Alabama, Lisa ran the business side of it. We had payroll to meet, we had employees who counted on us, and hundreds of patients to care for. So even though we had no idea how we'd get through it, we stood up and we slogged ahead, one step at a time.
>
> Somebody sent us Psalm 126:5–6 (ESV):
>
> Those who sow in tears
> shall reap with shouts of joy!
> He who goes out weeping,
> bearing the seed for sowing,
> shall come home with shouts of joy,
> bringing his sheaves with him.
>
> That message was important to us: *Even though you're crying, you've got to work in the fields now, because later, you'll need that harvest. God will bless it.* So we went back to work way before we thought we could, and God gave us the strength every day. We would come home and collapse into each other's arms.
>
> We had a teenage daughter, a junior in high school at the time, living with us. We said to each other, "Kayla's got to

finish high school. We have to hold ourselves together to see her through it." Kimber, our middle daughter, was just getting engaged. Josh, our oldest son, was devastated by the loss of Mitch, and yet he still had work and college. And our oldest daughter, Caitlyn, was the one who had just had a baby. We had to go share that experience with them and find some way for that to be a happy time of welcoming a new family member. Caitlyn and the baby deserved that.

It was almost a cacophony of sorrow and joy. From devastating loss on one hand to great joy and gain on the other. It was too much to take, and yet we didn't have the luxury of doing what we felt like doing—just lying down and dying.

I know that some marriages fall apart after the loss of a child, and I understand the emotional devastation that causes that. But for me, the experience made me treasure and value and cherish Lisa more, because she was there for me. She was so kind to me throughout the process—she would recognize those moments when I needed to be propped up. And at other moments I would see that she needed to be held up. I'm amazed to be able to say it, but our marriage never struggled as a result of this. It made us stronger.

Lisa said:

I know that's not typical. But I think the fact that Lee and I worked together in Lee's practice helped us create the kind of relationship that allowed us to deal with Mitch's loss and come out stronger on the other side of it.

Many people, such as our employees, some of whom weren't Christians, noticed that we didn't give up, that we kept going—that, in fact, we still had joy. That's life, after all. You *will* have tragedy. That's been promised. But even so, you get to choose: *Will I still have joy in spite of my circumstances?* We did, because that's the choice we'd made.

Of course, joy wasn't *all* we felt. For a while, I became depressed. I hid it from our employees, my friends, my kids, even Lee. They knew I was sad, but they didn't know how bad it had gotten. I had never before experienced real depression. A lot of my symptoms were spiritual. What I was experiencing was in fact spiritual warfare. I grew up in a home in which belief in God was a given—anything else would have been unthinkable. Now I found myself sometimes doubting that he existed. It was profoundly upsetting to me.

Lee:

For my part, I had a lot of anger. I felt cheated. I felt like it had been a trick. Mitch and I had *just talked* on the phone and worked out a plan for him to come home. He sounded warm, even relieved. Why would God play it out that way? Why make it seem like it was going to be okay—and then it wasn't okay? I felt debilitating grief—but I also felt anger.

God is sovereign, I knew, and he can do things as he sees fit. But that he would see *this* as being okay—I struggled with it both emotionally and intellectually.

It took me a long time to work through that. For me, coming to terms with it involved that conversation Jesus has with the disciples in John 6:66–69 where he says something to the effect of, "Everybody's leaving me. Are you guys going to leave me too?" And Peter replies, "Where would we go? Nobody but you has the words of eternal life." And I realized, *Okay, I can be as angry as I want, but at the end of the day, there's no other place to go.* And even though I didn't feel it right then, I had just enough faith to know that holding on to the Lord was still the answer.

How did the experience change us? Well, we don't let things go when there's turmoil or any kind of strife. We deal with it. For lack of a better phrase, we'll pick the scab every time. We don't let the sun set on our wrath, and we try to deal with things in real time, because we know there's no guarantee that we'll still have the opportunity the next day.

It brought us closer together. I don't know really how to explain that other than the Lord's involvement.

Lisa:

And you realize that what you might think is important really isn't. The real things in life—meaningful relationships, literally taking every day as a gift—are what's important. We don't take anything for granted, and that includes each other. I walk Lee out to his car every morning when he leaves for work—and we live in Wyoming now, so that can be kind of a big deal since I'm usually still in my pajamas with no shoes on! You just can't take anything for granted, and we don't, ever.

Lee:

One big bottom line for us was learning to separate our sense of purpose and our sense of joy from our circumstances, and learning not to let a moment slide without trying to make things right with the people we love.

One other bottom line. A big one. You just keep going. You get up, you try, as much as possible, to have a normal life. Things *aren't* normal, and your life will never be the same again, but it's still life—it's still going on. And eventually one day, like with us, we just realized, *We had a good day. Like, all day, we didn't cry, didn't get sad.* And that was because day after day, week after week, month after month, we just kept going. Kept doing what needed to be done. We didn't curl up into a ball. We didn't give up. We just kept going.

Discussion Questions
for Couples and Small Groups

1. What change do you want to make after reading this chapter?
2. Lisa and Lee Warren found great comfort in Psalm 126:5–6 (ESV):

    Those who sow in tears
        shall reap with shouts of joy!
    He who goes out weeping,
        bearing the seed for sowing,
    shall come home with shouts of joy,
        bringing his sheaves with him.

    Discuss how those verses might apply to the current and recent crises and sorrows in your marriage.
3. This chapter suggested that "the challenges of life and marriage are much the same. Those challenges are 'life's gym.' They're your workout. And the goals are building a stronger, healthier marriage and family, finding a new normal, and not letting life defeat you." Identify some of the challenges in your life that qualify as your workout, and discuss how, regardless of how painful and trying they are, they're making you stronger and healthier.

4. This chapter encouraged you to put these principles to work:

   Keep your eyes on the prize.

   What doesn't kill you makes you stronger.

   The fact that things are getting tough is no reason to give up.

   Stay flexible.

   Give yourselves credit.

   Recognize that some life challenges can never be completely overcome.

   Which of those are you best at? Which do you need to work on?

CHAPTER 11

Kissing the Scars

Like the spine of a good book, scars, by their very nature, imply there's a story to tell. They represent a wrinkle in time in which a person's life is changed forever, and they serve as permanent reminders of an incident that, in one way or another, has made a lasting impression on one's life.

—Sharon Jaynes

My first life lesson in the role of scars in our lives was taught to me by my son, Ben. I (Cindy) was a first-time mom of a nine-year-old adopted son, and Ben was giving me a crash course on the world of boys. I'd grown up in a girls' world with one sister and a slew of mostly girl cousins, so I had no idea until I was suddenly parenting Ben that comparing scars was a getting-to-know-you ritual of elementary-age boys.

"How many scars do you have?" Ben would ask of a new friend in the back seat of the car on the way to the park.

The first time I heard him ask, I laughed to myself, thinking, *What kid knows the answer to that question*?

"Eleven," came the instant answer. "How about you?"

So much for what I knew about boys.

"Nineteen. I got a new one two weeks ago on my arm. See? I can't tell if it'll fade away or not."

"What's your longest one?"

"This one on my elbow, but my favorite is on my foot from a nail that went straight through my shoe." I could see in the rearview mirror that the shoe and sock were coming off.

"Awesome," came the commentary.

Who knew what a great conversation starter scars could be? The scar talk consumed much of the drive time as the boys swapped stories of their injuries. There were snakebites, bike accidents, playground wounds, camping mishaps. Every scar had a story to tell.

Since Ben had just moved into a new family, neighborhood, school, and church, every friend was a new friend, so I heard the tour of scars multiple times. It never failed to jumpstart a lively conversation, and I quickly caught on that in a boy's world, scars were not only a trusty conversation starter but also a badge of honor.

Then one night, Ben's youth pastor brought him home early from a youth group camping trip with a long, jagged, deep wound that spanned his knee cap and then some. The ugly, gaping gash must have been at least five inches long. Off to the emergency room we went with Ben in considerable pain. He was putting on a brave face until the doctor prepared to insert a very large needle into the wound. Ben feared needles—hated them with a passion. He resisted and fought back fearful tears.

"It's just a local anesthetic," the doctor explained. "It will stop all the pain while I clean and stitch up the wound." Ben wasn't buying it and refused the shot. Seeing that a wrestling match was about to ensue, the doctor turned and looked at me, back in the corner of the ER examining room where I'd been trying to stay out of the way of the nurses and doctor. What to say? And then I thought of all of Ben's scar talk.

"Doctor," I said, "is this going to leave a scar?"

"I'm afraid so," the doctor answered. "A considerable one, right across the knee cap and below."

I saw Ben's face light up a bit.

"Ben," I said in as encouraging a voice as I could find, "you're going to have an awesome scar. If you let the doctor numb your knee, you can watch as he stitches it up. Think of telling *that* story to your friends." Ben stopped squirming and considered this. I could see the wheels turning. "I'll hold your hand while he does it," I promised.

Ben assented. Crisis averted. No battle scene to endure. My hand got crushed for the next few seconds, but the anesthetic took effect quickly and soon Ben was so fascinated at painlessly watching the doctor suture his wound that he dropped my hand completely. It wasn't long before the knee scar won all contests for best scar in the car.

Lesson learned: Every gaping wound is a scar in the making, with a story to tell.

Redeeming the Scars Together

Fast-forward eight years to the year 2000. I'd picked up a few scars of my own by then—from an ovarian cyst, a ruptured ectopic pregnancy, two renal surgeries, and so on. But the physical scars paled in comparison to the emotional scars I now bore, most notably from the many wounds that accompanied an unwanted divorce, subsequent severe depression, and the pain of abandonment with its loss of trust, of family, of home.

Then I began to date Dave Lambert. Dave and I were fifty-two and forty-two and as with any couple who doesn't start dating until later in life, we each had a lifetime of stories to tell one another. By human standards, we both had cause to never give such trust to a person again, but we could sense that the trust growing anew in both of us was not a human trust mustered from within ourselves, but an overflow of the trust God had instilled within us. He'd been faithful in our past and would be faithful in our future, and we realized slowly that we could actually trust the gift of love he was growing between the two of us.

So we shared the joyous stories of our lives—the stories of our coming to faith, of first loves and births and adoption, of life's many opportunities and jobs and ministries and friendships. But we also shared our scars. Tentatively at first, then more and more until the trust had grown so much between us that we flooded each other with the stories of pains and losses, betrayals and deaths, tears and rejections. Such scars were the evidence of God's faithfulness because rather than being open, raw sores, they had become scars of past wounds in various stages of healing and fading.

We married in 2002. I will never forget one night when we were newly married. We were lying in bed in each other's arms when I first noticed a small scar on Dave's chest. "That's from my leukemia days," he said. "I needed a port for the chemo." He proceeded to tell me more about his battle with leukemia than he ever had before. Moved by the pain and suffering he'd endured as he'd fought for his life, I caressed his scar, then kissed it.

Then I pulled back the sheets and touched the scar on my abdomen. "This is from my ectopic pregnancy," I said, concentrating so that I would be able to speak through emotions that were still strong, even years after the fact. "I prayed for that child for a decade. There was nothing I wanted more than a newborn child of my own. I believed God had designed me to be a loving mother, but years of infertility had left me confused and longing. All my life, from the time I was a little girl playing with dolls, I looked forward to becoming a mom. When I lost that baby—not even knowing whether it was a boy or a girl—I felt such bleakness, such despair. Such grief."

Dave ever so slowly and tenderly kissed my scar.

For the next hour we slowly revealed to one another physical scar after scar and kissed each one. We shed tears together. These were holy moments between a husband and wife, symbolic of embracing one another's pains and losses, of sharing the wounds we'd both suffered—physical and emotional and spiritual—and the healing that followed each wound.

We named that night *the kissing of the scars*. To this day, it remains one of life's most precious moments for us both, and not only do we refer to it in new times of duress and suffering, but sometimes in circumstances of great pain or loss we repeat the kissing of the scars as a way to offer empathy and healing to one another.

Dave and I have found that understanding the nature of wounds and scars in a marriage can add great strength to our relationship and build considerable staying power over the long haul. Facing the many crises of life leaves scars on our souls. But scars are a beautiful thing, for they are healed wounds, each scar telling a story of God's faithfulness at work in our frailty. After all, as Psalm 147:3 says, "He heals the brokenhearted and binds up their wounds."

Scars versus Open Wounds

There is a vast difference between an open wound and a scar. As Ben's experience in the ER shows, open wounds are painful, vulnerable to infection, and in need of cleansing, treatment, and dressing for protection. Scars, on the other hand, are healed wounds. Either we can see them as ugly tissue that mars our skin, or we can see them for the beautiful thing they are—evidence of an old problem solved, an old crisis now healed, a much-needed intervention where it was necessary to cut in order to heal. Our physical scars are a visible map of God's healing intervention in our lives. So, too, are the emotional and spiritual scars we bear from the pains and losses and healing of the past.

As in the kissing of the scars, a couple can use their open wounds—emotional, physical, and spiritual—as touch points of compassion and tenderness and reminders that our raw wounds will one day be healthy scars symbolic of God's past faithfulness.

Remember Brad and Carrie and Troy and Katie and Paige from chapter two, the family threatened by Troy and Katie's drug addiction? Their story illustrates how an open wound—a life crisis while it's still happening—gives us a choice to make. How will we handle our open wounds *together* so they heal into healthy scars we share rather than festering into deeper wounds that tear our marriage apart?

In chapter two, we saw how Troy and Katie's addictive behaviors eventually resulted in Brad and Carrie having to step in on behalf of their granddaughter Paige. But an earlier episode, when their son Troy was in his late twenties, is instructive as well. At that point, after a roller coaster of interventions and rehabs, tough love, and tender care, Troy and Katie still found themselves jobless, carless, and homeless—not only broke, but broken. Brad and Carrie talked at great length about whether to do anything to help them, and if so, what they should do. Those were not easy conversations. But in the end, they called Troy and Katie. "Troy, you need help," Carrie said, "and we know of an inpatient rehab program up near us that takes six months. If you agree to enroll in that program and to stay in it until your counselor says you're done, then Katie and Paige can move in with us until you graduate."

And so Katie and Paige moved in. Troy entered rehab.

Nothing about the situation was easy. Katie, depressed and bitter, spent most of her time sullen and in bed, leaving Carrie to handle the bulk of Paige's care. When Troy had been in rehab for only a month, he wanted out. "Really, my counselor says it's all right," he lied. "He says I've made such great progress I don't really need the rest of the program." Katie also wanted Troy to leave rehab and instead use outpatient care so he could get a job and save enough to get out on their own again. Against the pleading of Brad and Carrie, Troy left rehab and joined Katie in Brad and Carrie's finished basement.

Filled with grief and heartache, Brad and Carrie watched this recovery attempt unravel before their eyes. Troy did get a job—but his frequent absences from work aroused their suspicions that he was using drugs again. Katie was still staying in bed all day. Troy and Katie argued whenever Troy was home, creating stress and tension throughout the house. There was a lack of daily routine for Paige unless Carrie stepped in to try to provide it by taking her to preschool, structuring bedtimes and bath times, and providing family meals, all of which caused tension with Katie. Troy and Katie took to arguing outside, where the neighbors could hear screaming and crying. Tensions among the four adults over the handling of household chores, smoking, and the use of foul language went unresolved. Money seemed to mysteriously disappear; Brad and Carrie found themselves hiding their wallets and packing away valuables so they wouldn't be stolen for drug money. Their prescription medications had to be locked up or they, too, would mysteriously disappear.

Brad and Carrie struggled to agree on how to respond. How much should they intervene? In what ways? Should they take on more daily decisions for Paige's care while under their roof? How much should they allow the dysfunction of addiction to rule over the daily functioning of their household? Should they establish healthy boundaries to keep their home a safe and sane sanctuary, and if so, what boundaries? Should they tell Troy and Katie to leave? Where would they go, and what would become of little Paige?

"I just feel like this is Troy's last chance," Carrie told Brad, "and I can't bear to see him fail at it. I know what a struggle it is for you—but I keep thinking that maybe in a week, or two, or a month, something will click in for him. He and Katie both have such an unhealthy, self-destructive lifestyle now. For their sake and mostly for Paige's, who didn't ask for any of this and didn't do anything to bring it about, I just want to help them find a healthier relationship free of substance abuse. As long as they stay here, then at least they're being exposed to a model of a loving Christian home. And if all Troy will agree to is outpatient care, then at least I can support him in that."

"I know," Brad said. "But I can see the toll it's taking on you. I see every day how you grieve as the evidence piles up that, rather than our home becoming a safe haven and a healing place for them, in reality they have no interest in creating new patterns of behavior. Call it ignorance, call it stubbornness, call it lack of will or ability, whatever the cause, Troy and Katie aren't just continuing all their destructive patterns, they're transforming our home into another dysfunctional environment, and there's nothing we can do to stop it as long as they live here."

Brad and Carrie each worried about the toll this situation was taking on the other and on their own marriage. Brad grew steadily more angry—angry at Troy for his lack of resolve to change and at Katie for her perpetual laziness and hostility toward them all. He watched his wife try so valiantly only to have her every effort to help backfire. How long should he allow this dysfunction to continue to take its toll on his wife and their home and their finances before he pulled the plug? Or should he wait for Carrie to draw that same conclusion? What would Jesus want him to do?

Even though they approached it from very different perspectives, Brad and Carrie both recognized that their home situation was an open wound and that both of them were suffering because of it. They could have responded to that in many different ways, some of them constructive and some of them destructive. Marriages have foundered on less. Brad and Carrie's decision was to treat one another with tenderness through the daily pain. In the privacy of their own bedroom, they invited the other to speak about their perspective. When the other was speaking, each worked hard to listen attentively, to provide comfort and empathy, and to discuss and pray about the next day's action steps. They took the long view: this wound would need to be cleansed and treated before it could begin to heal, and that would take time. They each committed to be there for the other, to stitch the wound with tenderness rather than tear it further apart. It wasn't easy.

"The thing is," Brad said, "every day we have to make some decision about how to react to some new outrage or where to draw a line in the sand. And I'm never sure whether we're right or wrong, wise or unwise. Not once. There's no manual for this sort of thing. We just take our best shot and try to decide what's best for everybody, and are we right? Wrong? Who knows? And that's stressful in itself."

The one thing they did know was that they were determined to tend this wound together.

When the six months were up, the question of whether to allow Troy and Katie to stay was resolved for them. One night, they heard shouting from the basement, then Troy came upstairs and announced that they were leaving for Katie's parents' home a couple of states away for a long weekend and would like to borrow one of Brad and Carrie's cars for the trip. "We'll be back on Monday. We promise," he said. An hour later the weary parents waved goodbye to Troy, Katie, sleepy little Paige, and their car.

Monday came and went. On Tuesday they got a call from Troy: "Katie refuses to come back and I won't leave her. But we'll return your car as soon as we can borrow another one." That day never came. Three months later, Brad and Carrie made the long round trip to retrieve their car. They said a heartbreaking farewell to their granddaughter and an awkward goodbye to Troy and Katie and drove back to their now quiet home.

Now came the work of dressing the wounds they both carried. Carrie was heartbroken, realizing that all of their efforts, all of their investment of time and money and love and comfort had apparently accomplished nothing—Troy and Katie's situation was unchanged. Brad was relieved to have his house back but worried over Carrie's sadness. They both worried about Paige.

It took about six months more before they could acknowledge to each other that their open wound was finally scarring over. That was twelve years ago. Today Brad and Carrie, still a couple highly committed to each other, intentionally celebrate the scar they bear from that period of their lives. When they discuss that painful trial, they can see God's faithfulness to them through it all. They can celebrate the support they gave one another in spite of the confusion, chaos, and pain of the daily struggles of that six months.

They mutually recognize that in her desire to host what she hoped was her son's recovery, and in her stubborn and constant support for Katie and Paige, Carrie was following the example of Jesus to sacrificially pour out her life and her love, and that was the right thing to do regardless of how it turned out. They recognize Brad's strength and leadership in supporting her in that decision, even though he himself was torn. And they acknowledged his willingness, when torn between love and justice, to allow love to win out. They give thanks that God protected them as a couple during that time period (and the years before and after)—that they didn't devolve into criticism and conflict with one another but, instead, stayed united even though their perspectives were different.

Though Brad and Carrie's help had not proven to be the solution for Troy and Katie's problems, their efforts were a factor, a stepping-stone, in Troy's recovery journey. Troy did eventually break free from his addictions and lives today as a recovering addict.

Today, Brad and Carrie's "scar talk" recognizes and celebrates all that unfolded during that difficult episode of their life, which builds their faith for the next trial they will endure as a couple. And their willingness to share their story with other couples, and even to share it with us in this book, is an example of the value of scar talk. Such vulnerable honesty encourages others to remain sensitive and loving when dealing with open wounds and to stay focused on seeking God's wisdom.

Scar talk is all about acknowledging God's work in the midst of our wounds, his healing of the scars left behind by those wounds, and his faithfulness in the midst of our human frailty.

So reveal to one another your scars—old wounds now healed—and kiss them, telling the story of God at work in your healing.

Also, kiss and bind up your open wounds together, confident that no matter how deep and ugly the wound, it, too, will one day be a healed scar.

Finally, remember that your Savior also bears scars.

By His Wounds We Are Healed

And that is perhaps the most important role that our wounds and scars play in our lives—to remind us that our Savior did not leave us alone to suffer the consequences of our own sin and the sin in this broken world. We are loved by a wounded, scarred Lord. As Scripture says, "'He himself bore our sins' in his body on the cross, so that we might die to sins and live for righteousness; 'by his wounds you have been healed'" (1 Pet. 2:24).

I believe that one of the most tender moments in the New Testament is found in the Gospel of John. Place yourself in this scene described by John, who lived it. As you read, consider the intimacy shared between Jesus and his disciples in this scene. Remember that Jesus had just been raised from the dead that very morning.

> On the evening of that first day of the week, when the disciples were together, with the doors locked for fear of the Jewish leaders, Jesus came and stood among them and said, "Peace be with you!" After he said this, he showed them his hands and side. The disciples were overjoyed when they saw the Lord. (John 20:19–20)

Can you see it—Jesus opening his robe in front of them and revealing his side? Jesus stretching his hands out to his friends and them all drawing near to see and touch for themselves. These were sacred wounds, borne for them and for us. Although the passage doesn't specify the wounds' condition, I have always imagined Christ's wounds as still open but no longer bloodied and painful. I can only imagine the wonder in the disciples' eyes and the tears that were shed in those vulnerable moments.

Poor Thomas, however, missed the event. He wanted to see the same proof for himself.

> Now Thomas (also known as Didymus), one of the Twelve, was not with the disciples when Jesus came. So the other disciples told him, "We have seen the Lord!" But he said to them, "Unless I see the nail marks in his hands and put my finger where the nails were, and put my hand into his side, I will not believe." (John 20:24–25)

I love what Jesus then did for Thomas's sake.

> A week later his disciples were in the house again, and Thomas was with them. Though the doors were locked, Jesus came and stood among them and said, "Peace be with you!" Then he said to Thomas, "Put your finger here; see my hands. Reach out your hand and put it into my side. Stop doubting and believe."
>
> Thomas said to him, "My Lord and my God!" (John 20:26–27)

Once Thomas touched those scars for himself, he understood that his own healing could begin.

If we choose to respond to the hand grenades life tosses into our marriage by using those occasions when life is tearing us apart to *build* our marriage, to strengthen it rather than allow it to be weakened, then we can determine to never again look at our wounds and scars the same way. Instead, we will reveal to one another every new open wound with the agreement that we want to be a part of the stitching process for one another. And we can share our scars with one another knowing they will be caressed and kissed because we have confidence that our grief, pain, and loss surrendered together to God become the holy ground of scars now healed. Let us build marriages on that holy ground.

Discussion Questions *for* Couples and Small Groups

1. What was your main take-away from this chapter?
2. Sharon Jaynes said, "Like the spine of a good book, scars, by their very nature, imply there's a story to tell." Share the story of one of your scars—a past loss that is now healed. What most helped that wound to heal?
3. Identify an open wound in your life—an area of pain or loss that is still in need of healing.
4. Just as the gaping wounds of Jesus as he hung on the cross must have looked horrific, those same wounds were seen by the disciples, on the day of his resurrection, as beautiful evidence of Christ's ultimate victory. Thomas doubted at first until he saw the wounds in Christ's hands for himself. In what ways are you like Thomas?
5. At what point in your journey did you recognize God's touch in your healing? Share what happened.

CHAPTER 12

The Strength of Weakness

> My weakness, that is, my quadriplegia, is my greatest asset because it forces me into the arms of Christ every single morning when I get up.
>
> —Joni Eareckson Tada

What is your greatest asset as a couple?

Perhaps you, like the Kents and the Lamberts, are inclined to answer that question by thinking through your greatest strengths. But Joni's challenging quote, above, stopped us in our tracks. It had never occurred to the four of us to name our weaknesses as our greatest asset. Yet, as Joni points out, it is our weaknesses that drive us into the arms of Christ. And surely, there is no more powerful place to be than wrapped in the arms of our Lord and Savior.

No one likes to feel weak or powerless. Isn't this one reason we shudder when a crisis hits? Who wants to face circumstances that are overwhelming, challenges that are crushing, obstacles that are staggering? We all prefer feelings of strength, competency, and being in command. But when a crisis hits, we don't have a choice. The only way through it is forward, ready or not. And *not* is how we usually feel at such times.

And yet the Bible makes it clear that something good can come of your feelings of weakness and powerlessness. Whatever your crisis, of this you can be certain: God is up to something. And even if the circumstances you must struggle through right now are horrific, the something he is up to is something *good*. Perhaps a new perspective on strength and weakness, power and powerlessness, could make a difference in your lives—not just in how you manage crises, but in creating a stronger marriage.

In 2 Corinthians 12:7, Paul is writing about what he called the "thorn in my flesh." He never tells us what it is, only that it causes him great suffering. Then in verses 8–10 he writes:

> Three times I pleaded with the Lord to take it away from me. But he said to me, "My grace is sufficient for you, for my power is made perfect in weakness." Therefore I will boast all the more gladly about my weaknesses, so that Christ's power may rest on me. That is why, for Christ's sake, I delight in weaknesses, in insults, in hardships, in persecutions, in difficulties. For when I am weak, then I am strong.

We believers get so used to hearing familiar verses that sometimes we respond to them numbly, just nodding and murmuring "uh-huh." But this passage is too important and too shocking for us to let ourselves respond that way. First, notice the *benefit* that Paul gets from his suffering, right after the words *so that*: "so that Christ's power may rest on me." And did he really say, "I delight in weaknesses," and "for when I am weak, then I am strong"?

Are you thinking, *I don't get it*?

We've been there. The Kents and the Lamberts have all four scratched our heads over these words when life hurts. How do our weaknesses result in God's power resting on us? How are we supposed to delight in weaknesses and difficulties? And how can we be weak and strong at the same time? Paul's perspective here sounds convoluted—completely the opposite of what seems reasonable or even comprehensible.

At first glance we might be tempted to wonder if Paul even knows what it feels like to be weak and powerless. He was a Pharisee, after all—a person of power. Could it be that he's just over-spiritualizing something he really hasn't known firsthand?

But a reading of the verses in context puts that question to rest. Paul wrote that puzzling passage from 2 Corinthians after having recounted for his readers what he'd been through *before* writing those words:

> I have worked much harder, been in prison more frequently, been flogged more severely, and been exposed to death again and again. Five times I received from the Jews the forty lashes minus one. Three times I was beaten with rods, once I was pelted with stones, three times I was shipwrecked, I spent a night and a day in the open sea, I have been constantly on the move. I have been in danger

> from rivers, in danger from bandits, in danger from my fellow Jews, in danger from Gentiles; in danger in the city, in danger in the country, in danger at sea; and in danger from false believers. I have labored and toiled and have often gone without sleep; I have known hunger and thirst and have often gone without food; I have been cold and naked. Besides everything else, I face daily the pressure of my concern for all the churches. Who is weak, and I do not feel weak? Who is led into sin, and I do not inwardly burn? If I must boast, I will boast of the things that show my weakness. (2 Cor. 11:23–31)

Yes, Paul clearly *did* know what it was to be weak and powerless. He'd had far more practice at it than most of us. How then can he talk about delighting in weakness?

We have a big, audacious prayer request for you, our reader, in this final chapter. We pray that you begin to embrace Paul's perspective as your own. We have. But not until we'd been face-to-face with the impossible for some time. Not until we, too, were thrust into powerlessness and forced to operate in our weakness.

Choices in Times of Weakness

As we've traveled these chapters together, the stories we've told and comments we've made have probably unearthed in your mind memories of times you found yourself powerless to overcome the challenges of life. Times when you experienced grief, anger, or discouragement. We hope we've stirred your faith in the midst of such memories so that as the future unfolds, you will be emboldened at the first signs of "weakness" to run full speed into the arms of Jesus. There your faith can move you to make choices that, even in your powerlessness, can empower you to overcome the obstacles before you.

Ask for God's help in your weakness.

> In the same way, the Spirit helps us in our weakness. We do not know what we ought to pray for, but the Spirit himself intercedes for us through wordless groans. (Rom. 8:26)

Knowing this truth, when we feel undone we can pray, acknowledging our feelings of powerlessness. It can be as simple as, "Lord, help us." Prayer is an act of faith and submission to God. This verse is a powerful reminder that it's okay that we don't even know what we need most, for God does. The Holy Spirit himself intercedes—communicates to God—on our behalf at a depth too great for words.

Honor God's omniscience and mystery.

Why does God allow these things—the financial challenges, the health struggles, the family troubles, the trauma? We can't answer that any more than you can—but we hope that, like us, you cling to the truth that God is holy, in control, and filled with lovingkindness. Just because we can't comprehend God's ways in whatever tough situation we face doesn't mean we can't cooperate with God. Allow this verse to remind you that God has an eternal perspective for what he is accomplishing in and through your life.

> "For my thoughts are not your thoughts, neither are your ways my ways," declares the LORD. "As the heavens are higher than the earth, so are my ways higher than your ways and my thoughts than your thoughts." (Isa. 55:8–9)

Often when a crisis hits we expend energy wondering *why* and trying to make sense of what seems senseless. This verse reminds us that *why* is above our pay grade. Cling, together, to the truth that God is at work, even when you cannot imagine how.

Surrender to God's will.

Is surrendering to God's will easy? Not at all. It wasn't easy for Jesus in the garden of Gethsemane either. He agonized in prayer over it, but then finally:

> He went away a second time and prayed, "My Father, if it is not possible for this cup to be taken away unless I drink it, may your will be done." (Matt. 26:42)

He surrendered. Let's follow Jesus's example.

Watch for evidence of God's grace and power at work in you and through you in the midst of your crisis.

> "My grace is sufficient for you, for my power is made perfect in weakness." Therefore I will boast all the more gladly about my weaknesses, so that Christ's power may rest on me. (2 Cor. 12:9)

The Power of Surrender

Some of Jesus's followers expected him to enter Jerusalem not on a donkey but with an army to set Israel free from its occupation by the Romans, to enter not as a suffering savior but as a king, to enter not in humility but in power. And yet his choice was the necessary one—to present himself as a sacrifice, despite having the power that created the universe at his disposal. He could have called ten thousand angels, and yet he presented himself as an example of weakness and powerlessness. God, the Almighty One, in the ultimate display of his power and love sent his Son to hang naked on a cross and die there. Jesus more than anyone understood that "when I am weak, then I am strong" (2 Cor. 12:10).

I (Cindy) don't know what you are going through as a couple right now, but if you are a follower of Jesus I know this much: You have a Savior who, driven by his love for you, chose to exercise his holy, omnipotent strength in an act of unearthly surrender to his Father. And by that power he rose from the dead, securing your eternal salvation.

In God's economy, surrender to God is power and weakness is strength—even though, from an earthly perspective, that appears to us to be upside down and inside out. The values of the kingdom of heaven, as revealed in the Bible, and the values of this world are poles apart. In Matthew 20:20–23, the mother of two of Jesus's disciples, James and John, brought her sons to Jesus and asked that in heaven one of her sons be allowed to sit at Jesus's right hand and the other at his left. In his response, Jesus emphasized—one of the *many* places in the New Testament where he emphasized this—that in the kingdom of heaven, earth's values are turned upside down.

Predictably, the other ten disciples heard about James and John's mother's request:

> When the ten heard about this, they were indignant with the two brothers. Jesus called them together and said, "You know that the rulers of the Gentiles lord it over them, and their high officials exercise authority over them. Not so with you. Instead, whoever wants to become great among you must be your servant, and whoever wants to be first must be your slave—just as the Son of Man did not come to be served, but to serve, and to give his life as a ransom for many." (Matt. 20:24–28)

That's about as far away from the values of this world as you can get. The world preaches power—Jesus preaches powerlessness. The world wants to be master, wants to be first—Jesus preaches that you must become a servant, and that the one who wants to be first must instead become last.

Once, addressing a Christian businessmen's gathering, Dave decided to use the Sermon on the Mount in Matthew as his text. So as he discussed turning the other cheek, loving not just your friends but your enemies, and going the second mile, two lawyers in the room sitting near Dave turned to each other. One chuckled uneasily and stage-whispered, "We'd be out of business!"

Maybe so. If we all lived according to the values of the kingdom of heaven, power would lose its appeal to us. Rather than longing for power *over* our circumstances, let us long to have the heart of a servant *in* our circumstances. *Lord, how can I serve you in this horrendous situation?* Now that is power!

The Gift of Weakness

Remember Chad and Chloe from chapter 1? Chad lost his youngest brother in a car accident and tended to withdraw while grieving; his wife, Chloe, in her frustration at being shut out, had the habit of slapping the mattress to force communication between them. They finally turned to a counselor for help. They, too, experienced the power of strength in weakness. Their marriage remained difficult, and sometimes they doubted that it would last much longer. A year later things seemed to be going from bad to worse, and when they learned that Chloe would need a hysterectomy to put an end to her endometriosis, Chad feared that would be the last straw—a serious stressor that might be more than their marriage could stand.

After the surgery, he held her hand as she emerged from the anesthetic. She seemed subdued, a little teary. She remained in the hospital for a couple of days, and on the day she was released, she said, "After we get home you'll need to do some things for me that I can't do for myself. Do you think you're up to it? It won't be very pleasant."

He kissed her hand. "Whatever it is, I'll be up to it."

She smiled. He was encouraged, but also apprehensive. It wasn't unusual for Chloe to want to be waited on. But too often, her approach was to insist on it and get upset if it wasn't done in just the right way or on schedule. She resented her own weakness, and that made her want to reassert herself. Would that be true this time?

But she had seemed gentle in her request, and as the days went by, she remained gentle. And remained in bed as well. Her recovery was slow. Chad did indeed have to wait on her—to take care of the kids, do the cooking and the wash, and make sure she had food and beverages and her meds. He had to assist her with various personal tasks and procedures as well, and some might have considered those tasks, as she had forecast, *not very pleasant*. Chad, though, welcomed it. He had longed for years for the opportunity to do something, anything, that would ease the tensions between them. And now he had that opportunity. He waited on and served her in the most intimate and personal of ways, meeting her needs, doing for her the things she couldn't, in her condition, do for herself. The opportunity was created by her *weakness*. But it was made possible by her *meekness*. She allowed him to serve her.

Her approach hadn't been by design. She just sensed that allowing him to serve her needs and expressing appropriate thanks and appreciation for it was the best way for them both to get through it. And it was. It allowed them to improve their marital relationship without even trying to solve the many issues that had plagued them in the months and years before.

Would those issues have to be dealt with? Of course, and some of them were major. But when that time came, Chad and Chloe would be starting the process as a team, and on much better footing emotionally than at any time in recent memory. And all because, in her time of weakness, Chloe opened the door for Chad to serve her. Chloe's weakness had become, instead, something of great power.

We all remember the poem so popular a couple of decades ago, and still occasionally seen on posters and websites, called "Footprints." The one in which the narrator notices that in her walk with Jesus there were times when there was only one set of footprints on the sandy beach where they'd walked—not, as she first suspected, because Jesus had abandoned her. It was because at those times, he had carried her.

Our own times of weakness, just like Chloe's, can provide our spouse with the opportunity to follow Jesus's example. In your times of need, even if it makes you uneasy at first, let your spouse carry you.

As you look toward your unknown future as a couple, you, too, can choose the power of surrender. Take note of every weak and powerless thought and feeling the two of you have right now and offer them all to God to use as he sees fit—and he will bring true strength into your life. You *will* endure your current trial. You *will* survive it. You *will* grow stronger in him, richer in spirit, purer in heart.

Take a moment right now for one of you to read the following verses out loud. Do so with a prayerful heart that in your weakness, God will give you his strength.

> Brothers and sisters, think of what you were when you were called. Not many of you were wise by human standards; not many were influential; not many were of noble birth. But God chose the foolish things of the world to shame the wise; God chose the weak things of the world to shame the strong. God chose the lowly things of this world and the despised things—and the things that are not—to nullify the things that are, so that no one may boast before him. It is because of him that you are in Christ Jesus, who has become for us wisdom from God—that is, our righteousness, holiness and redemption. Therefore, as it is written: "Let the one who boasts boast in the Lord." (1 Cor. 1:26–31)

Today, put a stake in the ground. As you journey forward with your newfound staying power, determine that you will offer all your weaknesses and powerlessness to God for his use and his glory. And be confident of this: you will experience the strength of the Lord who loves you, the strength made perfect in our weakness.

And So, in the End, We're *Still* in This Together

That was how we started this book. It's in the title of the first chapter: *We're in this together*. Forgive us if we sound too familiar, but given the journey we've just completed together and the difficulty of some of the issues we've raised and memories we've conjured up, for you as well as for us, we like to think that *we*—meaning you, the reader, along with us, the authors—have been through something together.

Together we've investigated how to choose wisely and how to make some decisions ahead of time so that when the occasion arises, you already know what you'll do.

Together we've learned that anger, dangerous though it may be, also has its positive uses.

Together we've considered the importance of relaxation, even when times are tough, and of surprises and of automatic forgiveness.

Together we've heard the stories of some of those whose lives illustrate that even when deep in the throes of our own suffering, we can still serve others.

Together we've learned to be as stubborn as Winston Churchill: *Never give up!*

And together we've resolved that when the fights life sends us result in scars, we will celebrate rather than regret them.

Yes, we've been through it together—and as long as you're still working not just to preserve your marriage but to build it and strengthen it, to achieve ever deeper levels of intimacy, ever more equitable levels of mutual understanding, ever more mysterious levels of self-sacrifice on behalf of your spouse and your family, ever more intricate levels of communication (verbal as well as silent), ever greater moments of mutual appreciation and joy, then we, the authors, will continue to feel that we've created a bond with you that continues far beyond the moment you close the book's back cover.

Let the words of this passage, which we think of as the theme verses of this book, ring in your ears:

> Two are better than one,
>   because they have a good return for their labor:
> If either of them falls down,
>   one can help the other up.
> But pity anyone who falls
>   and has no one to help them up.
> Also, if two lie down together, they will keep warm.
>   But how can one keep warm alone?
> Though one may be overpowered,
>   two can defend themselves.
>   A cord of three strands is not quickly broken.
>   (Eccles. 4:9–12)

A cord of three strands . . . If you're blessed enough to be going through life as part of that set of three, celebrate your *staying power*.

Discussion Questions
for Couples and Small Groups

1. What one key idea in this chapter was the most helpful to you?
2. What about your situation makes you feel weak and powerless?
3. It seems paradoxical that God's strength and our weakness should be linked, as they are in 2 Corinthians 12:7–10. Can you think of examples, from your own experience or elsewhere, in which weakness became strength?
4. Where have you seen evidence of God's grace and power in your situation?

To Close Your Study
of This Book

Review the table of contents. Share one concept that has already begun to give your marriage staying power.

Appendix: Crisis Helpsheets

We realize that not every crisis a marriage faces can be responded to by reading a book, discussing it thoroughly between yourselves, and trying to gradually make some changes. Sometimes crises land hard and in a hurry:

Your aging parent, who has been living on his own, has a stroke and will need nursing care from this point on.

Your employer closes its doors unexpectedly and you're out of a job with no warning, no severance, no health insurance.

Your eighteen-year-old daughter sits you down and tells you that she's never been comfortable as a girl and that from now on she considers herself male, wants to be referred to by male pronouns, and wants to be called Nick.

You welcome a new baby into the world, still somewhat in shock that the baby was born with serious health challenges and unsure what this means for your future and for your family.

And so many other crises. We can't give you specific help with them all, but we have created thirteen crisis helpsheets that we hope will give you some direction on what to do first in an emergency and how to prepare for the long haul in thirteen different life crises. They also point you toward some other helpful resources.

Our prayers go with you!

CRISIS HELPSHEET 1:

The Chronic Illness or Disability of a Child

The emotional roller coaster of parenting children with a chronic illness or disability may include: loss, shock, anger, sorrow, impotence, fear, anxiety, guilt, decreased sense of self-worth, abandonment.

Of course, that's not everything. Parents also describe intervals of happiness, relief at finally having a diagnosis (*My child isn't dying!*), and hope (*If my child lives long enough, maybe the treatment picture will improve*).

These ideas may help:

- **Ask for what you need** from health-care professionals. You want clear and complete communication of both knowns and unknowns and to be fully heard as a custodial parent.
- **Take care of yourself.** Do everything healthy people need to do, *and* seek additional help as needed—especially mental health care if you experience signs of depression.
- **Help your disabled or ill children find their voices** to ask for what they need from you, from medical practitioners, and from teachers and siblings.
- **Equip your child to live with as much personal autonomy as possible.**
- **Understand the laws** protecting your child and family: Americans with Disabilities Act, Rehabilitation Act of 1973, Individuals with Disabilities Education Act, Patient Protection and Affordable Care Act, Supplemental Nutrition Assistance Program, Children's Health Insurance Program, Medicaid. Your state may have complementary laws and programs.
- **Find a tribe of parents** whose children live with disabilities or chronic illness—support and be supported, encourage and be encouraged, learn and grow together.
- **Learn to be an advocate.** Minnesota's Partners in Policymaking program offers advocacy resources and classes in twenty-six US states and six countries. Their handbook is free at http://mn.gov/mnddc/pipm/index.html.

Where to find more information: Check with the Minnesota Council on Developmental Disabilities, http://mn.gov/mnddc/resources/links.htm. Most other states have similar councils. Google the council in your state for local contacts.

CRISIS HELPSHEET 2:

The Death of a Friend or Loved One

As soon as you've lost a friend or loved one:

- **Don't critique your own feelings** or those of your spouse. Feel whatever you're feeling—shock, grief, relief, silence, anger, blame, disbelief, withdrawal—those are all normal reactions. Don't self-medicate to numb those feelings.
- **Search for ways to serve your grieving spouse** if one spouse was closer to the lost one. Give your spouse space, but don't hesitate to ask how you can help.
- **Share the news judiciously.** Give details as warranted, but resist the temptation to broadcast everything you know.
- **Be present.** Grieve with others in your circle who grieve. Tell stories about the one you've lost.
- **Clarify what's needed from you.** Don't make assumptions about who will do what in the first hours and days. As appropriate, ask for help and/or ask how you can help.
- **Pace yourself.** Don't isolate yourself from your spouse or others, and don't isolate yourselves as a couple. But *do* take time to decompress as needed. Eat, sleep, get fresh air.

Going forward:

Be aware of (and expect) the stages of grief identified by the psychiatrist and writer Elisabeth Kübler-Ross in her book *On Death and Dying* (New York: Touchstone, 1969):

Denial. Funerals and memorial services help combat this.

Anger. Anger is not the same as bitterness—it's an emotional component of grief.

Bargaining. No bargain with God will change things—but that's beside the point.

Depression. Some people get trapped here.

Acceptance. Acceptance keeps its own timetable. Bit by bit, it becomes possible to find a new normal.

Where to find more information:

- Aubrey Sampson, "Surviving the First Year after Losing a Loved One," The Disciple-Maker, March 8, 2019, https://thedisciplemaker.org/surviving-the-first-year-after-losing-a-loved-one
- Kathe Wunnenberg, *Grieving the Loss of a Loved One* (Grand Rapids: Zondervan, 2016)
- GriefShare: https://www.griefshare.org

CRISIS HELPSHEET 3:
The Loss of a Child

The loss of a child may be the most searing, complicated grief humans endure.

What to expect:

- Repeated bouts of disbelief, yearning, anger, sorrow, and resentment that your child is gone.
- Uninvited, sometimes disturbing, thoughts and images about the death of your child.
- Disappointment and anger over comments that are insensitive to your grief.

What to watch for:

- You may find yourself obsessing over your child's belongings.
- You may feel desperate to avoid people, places, and occasions that remind you of your child.
- Sounds, smells, tastes, and textures may overwhelm you with longing for your child.
- You may feel sad, guilty, bitter, isolated, or just numb.
- You may be tempted toward behavior or substances that produce numbness.
- Your spouse's grief may be different or on a different timetable.

What to talk about with your spouse:

- Talk about all of it.
- Share stories about your child. Laugh! Give thanks for the gift your child was and for all you had together—then weep over all you lost when you lost your child. Repeat.
- Admit any suicidal impulses or thoughts, and if either of you experiences them, seek care from a medical provider without delay.
- If after six months you're not functioning reasonably well in the normal routines of living—sleeping, waking, eating, bathing, dressing, engaging with friends, maintaining reasonable attention on normal tasks—discuss getting assistance from a mental health professional.

Where to find more information:

- Angela Miller, "7 Things I've Learned Since the Loss of My Child," *Still Standing*, https://stillstandingmag.com/2015/10/28/7-things-ive-learned-since-loss-child
- "Grieving the Loss of a Child," Coping with Cancer, https://www.cancer.net/coping-with-cancer/managing-emotions/grief-and-loss/grieving-loss-child
- Gary Roe, *Shattered: Surviving the Loss of a Child* (Wellborn, TX: Healing Resources Publishing, 2017)
- "The Death of a Child—The Grief of the Parents: A Lifetime Journey," https://www.ncemch.org/suid-sids/documents/SIDRC/LifetimeJourney.pdf

CRISIS HELPSHEET 4:

A Family Member's Health Challenge

In the face of suffering, loss, joy, and hope, remember these two great truths that exist in tension with each other:

Life is hard.
And God is good.

Hold on to that when you, your spouse, or a family member is sick or injured in a way that redirects the trajectory of your life together.

Listen. Be present and engaged with your loved one. Don't make assumptions. Ask open-ended questions such as: "Tell me how you're feeling." Then listen with care and full attention.

Talk. Don't make it about you, but don't withhold your sorrow, confusion, regret, frustration, apprehension, hope, determination, and commitment—seasoned with humility and grace. If you misspeak, ask for a do-over and try again.

Learn. Search out *reliable* sources to learn everything you can about your loved one's health issue. This will enable you to be an informed advocate.

Connect. Create a strong partnership with health-care providers and a solid support team of trusted friends and extended family.

Be realistic. Devise more than one plan: a *best-possible-outcome* scenario, a *this-will-take-some-adjustment* scenario, and a *this-is-really-tough-but-we'll-find-a-way* scenario. Ask: What resources will we need if this turns out to be long-term or permanent? Will we need to change our home? In what ways? What regular medical or social services do I need to arrange for? Then prepare to open a new chapter in your life that may be very unlike what came before.

Persevere. Determine that with God's help and with energy and imagination, you will do everything you can for as long as you can to care for the one you love.

Where to find more information:

- "Supporting a Spouse through a Health Challenge," Johns Hopkins Medicine, https://www.hopkinsmedicine.org/health/healthy_aging/caregiver_resources/supporting-a-spouse-through-a-health-challenge
- Erin Prater, "Chronic Illness in Marriage," Focus on the Family, https://www.focusonthefamily.com/marriage/facing-crisis/chronic-illness/chronic-illness-in-marriage

CRISIS HELPSHEET 5:
Surviving a Financial Crisis

How can you address a financial crisis with a minimum of damage to your marriage?

Be honest with yourselves. If you were misled or defrauded, say so. Admit mistakes, selfishness, gullibility. Make amends where you can. Forgive what you can. The serenity prayer is helpful here; pray it as you work on the crisis, especially if you or your spouse bears much of the responsibility for the situation.

Offer and ask for forgiveness as needed. Work with your spouse as a partner to find the best solutions and put them into practice. Congratulate each other for each step toward financial health.

Construct an accurate picture of your finances. List reasonable fixed monthly expenses for food, housing, insurance, transportation, and all assets; creditors will require this.

Don't make things worse by avoiding or lying to creditors. Speak with them straighforwardly about reducing monthly payments. Creditors don't want you to lose everything; they want you to pay them back.

Consider a reputable *nonprofit* debt counseling service. (Skip the for-profit ones.)

Increase your income with extra work or seek work that pays better. Sell luxuries to pay for necessities.

Control your pride. Collect unemployment if you qualify. In most states, the Health Insurance Marketplace saves money while mandating standards of care. Find out if you qualify for the Supplemental Nutrition Assistance Program.

Spend less. Downgrade cable; cancel memberships and subscriptions. Don't buy what you don't need; shop thrift stores first. Lower housing costs if you can. Sell a car. *Talk through all this with your spouse before taking any steps.*

Where to find more information:

- An extensive personal finances website, including information on getting out of debt: https://www.crown.org
- Michael R. Lewis, "How to Survive a Personal Financial Crisis," https://www.wikihow.com/Survive-a-Personal-Financial-Crisis

CRISIS HELPSHEET 6:

Alcohol or Drug Abuse by a Loved One

Alan Leshner, former director of the National Institute on Drug Abuse, characterized the essence of addiction as "uncontrollable, compulsive drug seeking and use, even in the face of negative health and social consequences."[1] Is your loved one habitually unable to maintain the normal routines of life because of compulsive drug or alcohol seeking and use? If so:

Action steps:

- **Find qualified treatment.** No matter who you are, you're probably too close to give your loved one the quality of help an unrelated expert can give. Start with your family doctor. You can also enter your zip code at https://www.findtreatment.samhsa.gov to find treatment options.
- **Look after yourself.** Ask people you trust for support and accountability.
- **Look after the children.** If there are kids involved, communicate what's going on at an age-appropriate level of detail.
- **Look after your assets.** Protect your property and financial assets from abuse by a loved one whose addicted behavior is out of control. Lock up money, alcohol, and prescription meds!
- **Look after your addicted loved one.** Addiction treatment is like cross-country hiking—we have to keep checking for True North and making course adjustments to end up where we mean to go.

If it was in your loved one's power to change to please and protect you, he or she would. Do what's in *your* power to support, encourage, and hold him or her accountable to own both the physical and the behavioral sides of treatment every day.

Where to find more information:

- National Institute on Drug Abuse (NIDA), *Principles of Drug Addiction Treatment: A Research-Based Guide*, 3rd ed. (CreateSpace, 2018)
- Gerald May, *Addiction and Grace: Love and Spirituality in the Healing of Addictions* (San Francisco: HarperOne, 2007)
- Treatment option: https://teenchallengeUSA.org
- Treatment for women: www.hovinghome.org

CRISIS HELPSHEET 7:
A Wayward Child or Adult Child in Crisis

Before things reach crisis stage:

- **See a doctor.** Regardless of your child's age, there are often treatable physical explanations for extreme behavior.
- **Don't blame yourself.** You might be the world's best parent (hint: none of us is) and still have a child with behavioral or emotional problems. Kids—like parents—make choices.
- **Remain strong,** for your child's sake and for the rest of your family. Get the support you need.
- Whatever the age of your misbehaving child, **remember that God loves your child more than you do.**

If it's an adult child in crisis you're dealing with:

- Remember that even the wise father in the parable of the prodigal son had a limited number of options, including two you share: **wait** and **pray.**
- Also like the father in the parable: **let them go** and **let them fail.** The prodigal son didn't come home until he had come to the end of himself.
- In the meantime, to protect your marriage and the rest of your family—**create appropriate boundaries.** Don't let one troubled and self-absorbed family member rule your home. Don't be an enabler.
- **Recognize that parenting options change with time even in the best of circumstances.** You'll always love your child, but sometimes your child's choices mean your influence as a parent is reduced before you're ready. Accept it and work toward a new relationship dynamic.

Where to find more information:

- Find a number of helpful articles at https://www.empoweringparents.com/articles
- Good advice on a variety of parenting topics—search for those related to your family's particular issues at https://www.focusonthefamily.ca/parenting and https://www.helpguide.org/children-family.htm
- Jim Hancock, *Raising Adults: A Humane Guide for Parenting in the New World* (Seattle: The Tiny Company Called Me, 2010)

CRISIS HELPSHEET 8:
Eldercare

Prepare before the crisis hits:

- Start the conversation! Find out what your parents' or aging relatives' preferences are and what they can afford.
- Take inventory: What are your aging loved ones' primary problems? Which are getting worse? What are their resources? What arrangements have they already made?
- Form the team that will help you: relatives, pastor, friends, doctors, elder law attorney.
- Investigate community support services and housing options in your area.
- Make a plan and review it with your aging relatives.

In a crisis, do these things first:

- First, consult with your aging relatives' doctors to see what steps must be taken immediately.
- If you already have a plan, notify all team members and put the plan into action.
- If your state has passed the CARE Act, talk to your doctor and hospital about it. (Find more information at www.AARP.org/supportcaregivers.)
- Take stock of what equipment (wheelchairs, walkers, oxygen, etc.) your loved one needs and arrange for it.

For the long haul:

- Care for yourself—you can't help your loved ones if you're falling apart.
- Seek out other caregivers and support groups; you're not alone.
- Both you and your aging loved ones need distraction and entertainment. TV? Music? Cable? Books and magazines? Buy them headphones!
- Acknowledge your feelings: worry, guilt, anger, resentment. Seek help if you need it.
- Find out what hospice options are available. Better too early than too late.

Where to find more information:

- HelpGuide: https://www.helpguide.org/home-pages/caregiving.htm
- AARP: https://www.aarp.org/caregiving
- US Administration on Aging provides a locator for eldercare, https://eldercare.acl.gov/Public/Index.aspx, and a thorough search engine for other resources in your area, https://eldercare.acl.gov/Public/Resources/Index.aspx
- Focus on the Family discusses at-home alternatives: https://www.focusonthefamily.com/family-q-and-a/life-challenges/at-home-alternatives-for-elder-care

CRISIS HELPSHEET 9:
Grandparents Raising Grandchildren

Day one—if you need to assume custody of your grandchild, do these things first:

- If your grandchild needs a car seat, borrow or buy one.
- Ask about current health issues; get a list of medications your grandchild is on and take existing prescriptions with you; get contact information for the child's doctor(s); get a simple consent-for-medical-treatment letter for the child, signed by the child's parent or legal custodian.
- Take a copy or photo of the child's birth certificate; get a signed power of attorney form to empower you to enroll the child in school; get the child's social security number.

Day two:

- If your grandchild is in school, visit or contact a school administrator and ask that teachers be notified of the custodial change.
- Contact CASA or the local probate court and ask for an appointment with a judge or social worker to ascertain your legal position with the child.
- Make an appointment for a physical examination for the child.

For the long haul:

- Find a lawyer.
- Take care of yourself, physically and mentally. Eat well, get some exercise.
- In addition to love, your grandchild may need counseling.
- Your grandchild may resent what they see as your part in the absence of the parent(s). Make time and space to work that out, even if it takes years.
- Encourage your grandchild to talk through feelings—listen carefully; fill in factual details as appropriate.
- If space is limited, get creative with room dividers to ensure appropriate privacy for your grandchild.
- If it's safe, encourage contact with your grandchild's parent(s)—include the absent parent(s) in events and milestones in the child's life.

Where to find more information:

- AARP provides a wealth of information for grandparents raising grandkids, including an assessment of legal needs. Start at: https://www.aarp.org/relationships/friends-family/info-08-2011/grandfamilies-guide-support.html
- HelpGuide: https://www.helpguide.org/articles/parenting-family/grandparents-raising-grandchildren.htm

CRISIS HELPSHEET 10:

Incarceration of a Loved One

If your loved one has just been arrested:

- First, choose an attorney (if you're not using a public defender). Find out:
  - » the likely cost of the defense
  - » bail options
  - » what the attorney will and will not do
  - » what to expect in court
  - » the likely timeline and sequence of events
- If your incarcerated loved one has children, immediately determine their location and status and your own rights and options concerning them.
- If your loved one requires medication, work through the lawyer and your loved one's doctor to make it happen.
- If you believe your loved one is being mistreated in jail, speak to your attorney, the American Civil Liberties Union, and your state's protection and advocacy agency.

Finding your new normal with a minimum of damage to your marriage:

- As frightening as it may be, you need to research and face up to what is coming and devise a plan for dealing with it—and that includes a budget.
- Be nonjudgmental toward your incarcerated loved one.
- Be an advocate for your loved one. Are there appeals to be made, officials or politicians to be approached?
- Network with others in your situation—consider joining or creating a support group.
- Ask family and friends for help when you need it.
- Decide how you want to tell others about your loved one's circumstances.
- If the emotional turmoil and stress seem overwhelming, consider counseling.

Where to find more information:

- Prison Fellowship: https://www.prisonfellowship.org/resources/support-friends-family-of-prisoners/coping-incarceration-loved-one
- Raising children with a parent in prison: https://www.prisonfellowship.org/resources/support-friends-family-of-prisoners/coping-incarceration-loved-one/raising-children-with-a-parent-in-prison
- Practical suggestions: https://www.wikihow.com/Deal-With-a-Loved-One-Going-to-Jail
- A wealth of helpful resources from InmatesPlus: https://inmatesplus.com (Be sure to click on your state at the bottom.)
- Carol Kent, *Waiting Together: Hope and Healing for Families of Prisoners* (Grand Rapids: Discovery House, 2016)

CRISIS HELPSHEET 11:

Infertility

Infertility is a different kind of crisis—it doesn't arrive suddenly, like a stroke. Instead, it can turn into an endurance contest. To make sure your marriage survives it:

Prepare for what's coming:

- You may experience feelings of failure or inadequacy, anxiety, loss, guilt, being judged, shame, jealousy, rejection or abandonment, loss of self-esteem, and anger. Don't judge yourself for those feelings! But do get help from your support system.
- You may experience financial stress. The costs of fertility treatments or in vitro fertilization can be high.
- Sex shouldn't be hard work, but it can feel that way when you're trying so hard to conceive.

To get through it and strengthen your marriage for the long haul:

- Be compassionate with your partner—and also yourself—as you wrestle with this life challenge together.
- Don't let infertility take over your life. Allow yourselves the occasional break from trying to conceive. Distract yourself with hobbies, exercise, travel, etc.
- Build a support network: friends, family, counselors, pastors, online or in-person support groups.
- Read up on the ways to give your body the maximum chance to conceive: tracking the timing of ovulation, foods to avoid or eat, etc.
- Start a journal of your quest to conceive.
- Exercise—move your body!
- Practice breathing techniques and meditation to deal with anxiety and stress.
- Remember that this, too, shall pass. Eventually, you will conceive, adopt, or adjust to the idea of an offspring-free life. One way or another, this time of struggle will end and you will move into a different phase of life.

Where to find more information:

- The National Infertility Association maintains a wealth of support and information: https://resolve.org. Also see: https://resolve.org/support/find-a-support-group.
- Matthew Arbo, *Walking Through Infertility: Biblical, Theological, and Moral Counsel for Those Who Are Struggling* (Wheaton, IL: Crossway, 2018)
- Infertility and marital problems: https://www.verywellfamily.com/how-infertility-impact-your-marriage-and-relationship-4121098

CRISIS HELPSHEET 12:

When Adopting or Fostering a Child Goes Wrong

Both adopting children and fostering them come with their own special challenges, even when everything goes great—and it rarely does. Research at Harvard and the University of Michigan reveals that kids who've been in foster care develop PTSD at *twice the rate of combat veterans.*

If you're just beginning your adoption or fostering journey—prepare:

- Make sure you're working with **a licensed, reputable agency** that can provide necessary education, training, and counseling.
- The children for whom you're providing a home will have issues of **abandonment, loss, and grief.** Give them space. Don't simply assume that they're happier now that they've left the chaos of their birth parents' home.
- Both you and your adopted/fostered children *will* have **expectations that aren't met.**
- Placement agencies make every effort to properly match children with parents who make a good fit. But **not every match is a good one.**
- **Birth parents sometimes change their minds**—especially if the birth mother and father aren't completely in agreement on the decision.

If things are already going wrong:

- **Ask for help.** Maybe none of the issues listed above will happen in your case—but all of them *may.* Many placement agencies offer counseling both before and after placement. Take advantage of it.
- Remember that foster children may have experienced abuse and trauma, and they may develop emotional or behavioral problems as a result. This is not their fault. **Be patient.** It's this very thing that you were called to.
- If you haven't already created a **powerful support system,** for both you and the kids, this is the time.

Where to find more information:

- Adoption help of many kinds: https://adoption.com
- Counseling: https://bethany.org/get-help/families
- iFoster's motto is: *Helping kids in foster care reach their full potential*; https://www.ifoster.org

CRISIS HELPSHEET 13:

Children Struggling with Sexual Preference or Gender Identity

Many Christian families are having to find their way through a bewildering array of sexual issues in today's world, from sexuality to gender identity—where *sexuality* refers to attraction and *gender identity* refers to a sense of self.

If your child is experiencing gender dysphoria—a strong tendency to identify as the opposite gender from their physical body:

- It may seem to come from out of the blue, but **your child may have been feeling this way for some time** and been reluctant to express it for fear of how it would be received.
- As parents, **remain flexible.** These are new issues for you but also for the medical world. Read widely, but hold it all loosely—you may read just the opposite next year.
- The Q in *LGBTQ* implies, among other things, that especially among adolescents, many folks test sexual orientation (attraction) and some conflate body dysphoria with gender dysphoria, and some feel stuck for a time if their families/friends overgeneralize or overcompensate while the individual is exploring.
- Remember that **every transgender person is different.** The treatment and support your child needs may be different from what his or her friends need.
- However bewildered you are—remember that **your child is having a tougher struggle than you are.**

For parents of LGBTQ children:

- No matter how shocked and pained you are, **maintain the bond.** Do not overreact; if you're angry, don't unleash that anger on your child. Let them know they are loved.
- **Encourage dialogue,** but start small lest they feel threatened. Ask to meet their friends, LGBTQ and straight.
- **Deal with it as a reality.** Don't assume it's just a phase.
- **Don't look to assign blame,** especially against your spouse: "If only you'd been more . . ."
- **Ask about bullying.** Many young people who identify as LGBTQ experience bullying at school and among their peers. Empathize. Advocate. Protect.

Where to find more information:

- Mark A. Yarhouse, *Understanding Gender Dysphoria* (Downers Grove, IL: IVP Academic, 2015)
- The Center for Faith, Sexuality & Gender specializes in helping churches and parents navigate these difficult waters: https://www.centerforfaith.com.
- Help for parents whose children come out as gay: https://www.embracingthejourney.org

Acknowledgments

What a journey writing this book has been! Our writing team is grateful to our publisher, the Revell division of Baker Publishing Group. We'd like to thank Lonnie Hull DuPont, Rachel McRae, Erin Smith, Gayle Raymer, and the entire Revell team for their encouragement and their careful attention to detail.

We are deeply indebted to the individuals and couples who contributed their stories and insights. We applaud and admire you for your honesty and transparency—thank you. This project would not have been possible without the true-life examples of staying power from the following people:

Lael Arrington (www.laelarrington.com) offers her audience help to live wisely in today's culture and to love well, with God's grace. She is the author of four books, most recently *Faith and Culture* (with Kelly Monroe Kullberg, Zondervan, 2011). On secular talk radio she cohosted a show interviewing comics and professors, surfers and scientists about what we believe and why we believe it. **Jack Arrington** has served as president of Houston Bible Institute, now the College of

Biblical Studies–Houston, and also as senior pastor of two churches for almost thirty years. He and Lael have been married forty-two years and are launching into retirement. They look forward to many more years of serving family and God's kingdom together.

Harriet and Dirk Buursma live in Grand Rapids, Michigan, where Harriet, a nurse, serves on the board of the Christian Learning Center and Dirk is senior editor-at-large at Zondervan, where he has worked for over thirty-three years. Both are Calvin College grads. In addition to Paul, parts of whose story you read in chapter 7, the Buursmas have two grown children and a granddaughter.

Kim Cusimano is a Christian teacher and author. Her poetry and articles have been published in several anthologies. Her greatest joy is being a wife and mother of four. As a mother to two special-needs adults, she spends her time encouraging those around her to reach their full potential and to enjoy the abilities God has given them.

Clare De Graaf is a follower of Jesus, an elder, a Bible teacher, and a blogger. For more than thirty years, he's been a full-time spiritual mentor of men all over the world—from college students to business and church leaders. Clare and his wife, Susan, live in Grand Rapids, Michigan, and are the parents of six children and grandparents of fifteen.

Bill and Pam Farrel are international speakers and relationship specialists with a focus on building up marriages and families. They cofounded Love-Wise, an organization that connects love to wisdom to provide practical insights for personal relationships. They are keynote speakers for marriage, family, men's, and women's events. Bill and Pam have authored over thirty-five books, including the bestselling

Men are Like Waffles and Women are Like Spaghetti (Harvest House, 2016). www.love-wise.com

Dan and Leigh Johnson live in the state of Washington. Leigh serves on the prayer team at her church and helps with the GriefShare Ministry. She enjoys writing and reading and is currently recovering from a total foot and ankle reconstruction of her "lucky leg." She eagerly anticipates the next chapter God has for her.

Kathy Knott and her husband, **Bob**, reside in Grand Rapids, Michigan. Using her gifts of empathy and compassion, Kathy has ministered to her patients as a nurse for forty-four years, including more than three decades in obstetrics and gynecology. She is also a bereavement specialist for patients who lose their babies. She has three grown children, a daughter-in-law, and six grandchildren.

Janet Holm McHenry (www.janetmchenry.com) is a speaker and author of twenty-four books, including *Prayer-Walk* and *The Complete Guide to the Prayers of Jesus*. Her business name is Looking Up! because she encourages others to look up in prayer. An avid prayerwalker, Janet has been featured widely in magazines, including *Health* and *Family Circle*. A former attorney, **Craig McHenry** is a full-time cattle rancher.

Kirsten Panachyda writes to infuse courage into the soul-weary. She is a speaker, Bible teacher, and award-winning writer. Kirsten blogs as www.kirstenp.com and is working on a book for parents of kids with mental illness. She and her husband, **Dan**, have two sons, and together they are a roller-coaster-riding, travel-loving, blue-hair-dyeing family.

Sarah Rollandini is the creator of Infertility Club, a Midwest ministry for women struggling with infertility. You can read her work in *The Penasee Globe*, christiandevotions.us, *Focus on the Family* magazine, and *Unlocked: Daily Readings for Teens*. Sarah became a mama through adoption and surrogacy and lives near Grand Rapids, Michigan, with her husband and their three children. www.sarahrollandini.com

Lisa and Lee Warren live in Wyoming, where Lee is a brain surgeon, inventor, Iraq War veteran, and writer. His first book, *No Place to Hide*, was named to the 2015 US Air Force Chief of Staff's Recommended Reading List. His newest is *I've Seen the End of You*. Dr. Warren has appeared on *The 700 Club* and the *CBS Evening News*, and his writings have been featured in *Guideposts* magazine. Lisa Warren is CEO of Warren Innovation LLC, a professional chef, interior designer, and a dedicated community servant and philanthropist. But her favorite job is spending time with her husband, their kids, and their three grandkids.

Brenda L. Yoder is a licensed mental health counselor, author, speaker, life coach, and host of the *Life Beyond the Picket Fence* podcast. She is a passionate communicator on life, faith, and family beyond the storybook image. Her newest book is *Fledge: Launching Your Kids without Losing Your Mind* (Herald Press, 2018). www.brendayoder.com

We also want to thank all of the contributors whose names do not appear on these pages—those whose names were changed for a variety of reasons. Often, for instance, use of their real names would have revealed truths about family members that would have complicated those individuals' lives. Those contributors were no less courageous in their willingness to relive with us difficult memories.

We would also like to thank Jim Hancock, veteran youth worker, filmmaker, and author, for advising us on the helpsheets that conclude the book and for writing many of them. Our helpsheets were inspired by and modeled after the Crisis HelpSheets for Youth Workers Jim created and offers through his website, www.thetinycompanycalledme.com /helpsheets. Thanks, Jim!

And finally, thanks to the many people who faithfully supported the four of us in prayer for the many months we worked together on this book. You are the secret, behind-the-scenes heroes of *Staying Power*. We believe there is great value in the wisdom and advice in these pages, but not because of the four of us whose names appear on the cover. If and when this book helps your marriage, chalk it up to the brave correspondents whose names appear above and to the prayer warriors who devoted hours to asking God to bless our efforts. We thank you!

Notes

A Note to the Reader

1. Ross Campbell and Dave Lambert, *Getting a Clue in a Clueless World* (Grand Rapids: Zondervan, 1996).

Chapter 1 We're in This Together . . . or Not

1. Syeda Ferguson, "Former Port Huron Man Faces Murder Charge," *Times Herald*, Port Huron, MI, November 24, 1999.
2. Carol Kent, *When I Lay My Isaac Down* (Colorado Springs: Navpress, 2013).

Chapter 2 Make the Next Right Choice

1. Clare De Graaf, *The 10-Second Rule* (New York: Howard Books, 2015), 71–72.
2. De Graaf, *The 10-Second Rule*, 72.
3. Point Man Ministries website is https://www.pointmankansas.org, or you can email Steve at pointmankansas@cox.net.
4. J. Randall O'Brien, *Set Free by Forgiveness* (Grand Rapids: Baker Books, 2005), 137.

Chapter 3 Anger Is Not the Enemy

1. Roy Milam, "Dealing with Anger in Marriage," Cornerstone Marriage & Family Ministries, accessed March 1, 2019, https://www.marriageministry.org/dealing-with-anger-in-marriage.
2. Jeremey Dean, "The Upside of Anger: 6 Psychological Benefits of Getting Mad," PsyBlog, March 6, 2012, https://www.spring.org.uk/2012/03/the-upside-of-anger-6-psychological-benefits-of-getting-mad.php.
3. Steven Stosny, "Anger in Marriage: Failure of Compassion and the Rise of Contempt," *Psychology Today*, November 4, 2009, https://www.psychologytoday.com/us/blog/anger-in-the-age-entitlement/200911/anger-in-marriage-failure-compassion-and-the-rise-contempt.
4. Milam, "Dealing with Anger in Marriage."

Chapter 4 Forgive Freely

1. See, for example, Dave Carder, *Anatomy of an Affair* (Chicago: Moody, 2017); and Willard F. Harley Jr., *His Needs, Her Needs: Building an Affair-Proof Marriage* (Grand Rapids: Revell, 2011).

2. GriefShare, https://www.griefshare.org.

3. Archibald Hart, quoted in James Dobson, *Dr. Dobson's Handbook of Family Advice* (Eugene, OR: Harvest House, 1998), 87.

4. Christian Care Connect, https://connect.aacc.net/?search_type=distance.

5. Lewis B. Smedes, *Healing the Hurts We Don't Deserve* (New York: HarperCollins, 1996), x.

6. "Forgiveness: Letting Go of Grudges and Bitterness," Adult Health, Mayo Clinic, November 4, 2017, https://www.mayoclinic.org/healthy-lifestyle/adult-health/in-depth/forgiveness/art-20047692.

7. "Forgiveness in Marriage—Quotes and Inspiration," January 8, 2018, https://www.marriage.com/advice/forgiveness/forgiveness-in-marriage-quotes-and-inspiration.

Chapter 5 The Right Word at the Right Time

1. Pam Farrel's story was adapted with her permission from "You Are Not Going to Like It," *Arise Daily Devos*, January 20, 2019, https://arisedailydevos.wordpress.com/2019/01/20/you-are-not-going-to-like-it/amp/?__twitter_impression=true, and from Bill and Pam Farrel, *10 Best Decisions a Couple Can Make* (Eugene, OR: Harvest House, 2008).

2. The movie *Unplanned*, directed by Cary Solomon and Chuck Konzelman (Scottsdale, AZ: Pure Flix, 2019), is based on the book by Abby Johnson and Cindy Lambert, *Unplanned: The Dramatic True Story of a Former Planned Parenthood Leader's Eye-Opening Journey across the Life Line* (Carol Stream, IL: Tyndale, 2014).

3. Gary Smalley and John Trent, *The Blessing* (Nashville: Thomas Nelson, 2011).

Chapter 6 An Articulate Silence

1. Gary Chapman, *The 5 Love Languages: The Secret to Love That Lasts* (Chicago: Northfield Publishing, 2015).

Chapter 7 The Power of Serving While Suffering

1. Lael Arrington writes and speaks on faith and culture. You'll find her blogs at http://www.laelarrington.com.

2. Kathe Wunnenberg, *Hopelifter* (Grand Rapids: Zondervan, 2013), 20. Find more information on Kathe Wunnenberg's books and ministry at http://www.hopelifters.com.

3. Tim Keller, *Walking with God through Pain and Suffering* (New York: Penguin Books, 2015), 58.

4. "Doing Good Does You Good," Mental Health Foundation, accessed March 1, 2019, https://www.mentalhealth.org.uk/publications/doing-good-does-you-good.

5. "Inspirational Quotes about Life," Christian Quotes for Reflection and Inspiration, accessed March 1, 2019, http://www.quoteschristian.com/life.html.

Chapter 8 Divine Surprises

1. Janet Holm McHenry, *PrayerStreaming: Staying in Touch with God All Day Long* (Colorado Springs: WaterBrook, 2005).

Chapter 9 Say Yes to Guilt-Free Time-Outs

1. Wikipedia, s.v. "guilt," last modified September 20, 2019, https://en.wikipedia.org/wiki/Guilt_(emotion).

2. If you haven't read Tim Hansel's excellent book by this same name, find a copy and read it! He makes a great case for us to relax without guilt as a way of recharging and preparing ourselves for whatever comes next. Tim Hansel, *When I Relax I Feel Guilty* (Chicago: David C. Cook, 1979).

3. You may want to check out Carol Kent's *He Holds My Hand* (Carol Stream, IL: Tyndale, 2017), a page-per-day devotional written by Carol for people who need fresh hope and renewed faith.

Chapter 10 Never Give Up

1. Winston Churchill, quoted by Frank Herron, "Never Never Never Give Up on CONTEXT for a Quotation," The Art of "Quotemanship" and "Misquotemanship," May 21, 2014, http://blogs.umb.edu/quoteunquote/2014/05/21/never-never-never-give-up-on-context-for-a-quotation.

2. M. Scott Peck, *The Road Less Traveled* (New York: Simon & Schuster, 1985), quoted at https://www.goodreads.com/quotes/34482-life-is-difficult-this-is-a-great-truth-one-of.

3. Marc Chernoff, "10 Hard Things to Remember When You Feel Like Giving Up," Marc & Angel Hack Life, October 7, 2018, http://www.marcandangel.com/2018/10/07/10-hard-things-to-remember-when-you-feel-like-giving-up.

4. W. Lee Warren, *I've Seen the End of You* (Colorado Springs: WaterBrook, forthcoming), 201–3.

Appendix: Crisis Helpsheet 6

1. Alan I. Lesher, "Addiction Is a Brain Disease," *Issues in Science and Technology* 17, no. 3 (Spring 2001), https://issues.org/leshner.

Carol and Gene Kent are the founders of Speak Up Ministries, which includes Speak Up Speaker Services, a Christian speakers' bureau; Speak Up Conferences, equipping the next generation of speakers and writers; and Speak Up for Hope, a nonprofit organization that benefits inmates and their families. Carol is an international speaker, and she has authored more than twenty books. Gene serves as chief operating officer of their ministries. They are both fans of tracking down the best cup of coffee in every city they visit, and their favorite activity is watching sunsets together.

Cindy and David Lambert have been influencing the Christian publishing world for decades, both as editors and as authors, having authored more than twenty books between them. Together they own Lambert Editorial, serving authors, publishers, and Christian ministries with their editorial and writing skills. They are the parents of six adult children, have nine grandchildren, and love to launch their kayaks together from the dock in front of their log cabin in Michigan.

Learn More about Carol and Gene

Carol and Gene Kent are the founders of Speak Up Ministries, which includes Speak Up Speaker Services, a Christian speakers' bureau; Speak Up Conferences, equipping the next generation of speakers and writers; and Speak Up for Hope, a nonprofit organization that benefits inmates and their families. Carol has authored more than twenty books, and Gene serves as chief operating officer of their ministries. They are both fans of tracking down the best cup of coffee in every city they visit, and their favorite activity is watching sunsets together.

CAROLKENT.ORG

@AuthorCarolKent

@Carol Kent

@CarolKentSpeaks

Learn More about
Cindy and David

Cindy and David Lambert have been influencing the Christian publishing world for decades, both as editors and as authors, having authored more than twenty books between them. They have six children and nine grandchildren and love to launch their kayaks together from the dock in front of their log cabin in Michigan.

Revell
a division of Baker Publishing Group
www.RevellBooks.com